THE
ACTION
woman
A–Z OF CONSUMER
RIGHTS

Other *Woman* books

The Best of *Woman* Fashion Knitting
The Best of *Woman* Family Cooking
The *Woman* A–Z of Family Health
The *Woman* Book of Beauty and Health

THE

ACTION

woman

A–Z OF CONSUMER
RIGHTS

Gaynor Morgan

Drawings by David Lock

GRAFTON BOOKS

A Division of the Collins Publishing Group

LONDON GLASGOW
TORONTO SYDNEY AUCKLAND

Grafton Books
A Division of the Collins Publishing Group
8 Grafton Street, London W1X 3LA

Published by Grafton Books 1988

British Library Cataloguing in Publication Data

Morgan, Gaynor
The Actionwoman A-Z of consumer rights.
1. Great Britain. Consumer protection—
Practical information
I. Title
381'.34'0941

ISBN 0-246-13195-0

Photoset by Rowland Phototypesetting Ltd
Bury St Edmunds, Suffolk
Printed in Great Britain by
William Collins Sons & Co. Ltd, Glasgow

PREFACE

'Actionwoman' has been in the forefront of consumer journalism since its launch in *Woman* magazine twelve years ago. Today, newspapers, magazines, television and radio have all taken up the cudgels of the consumer, while 'Actionwoman' continues to build on its strength, covering serious legal issues, giving guidance with personal finance, testing products from fizzy wine to microwaves, and bringing you up-to-the-minute consumer news affecting our everyday lives.

The world of consumerism is a wide one. In fact, almost everything we do involves consuming in some way or another, whether it's shopping, eating out, travelling, working, getting married or divorced, investing our money, buying a house or going to the doctor. The list is endless, as are the chances of something going wrong and the seriousness of the consequences. We might lose money, suffer an injury to ourselves or our property or just feel morally outraged. How often do you hear people say, 'They shouldn't be allowed to get away with it' or 'Something should be done about it.' Well, the law now favours the individual consumer more than ever before and so the chances are you *can* do something about it, if you know what, when and how. Even where the law can't specifically help, there might be some action you can take or pressure you can bring to secure a fairer deal.

The aim of this A–Z is to give basic advice and information and to tell readers what their rights are. While there has not always been space to go into great detail, I have pointed readers in the right direction and then suggested where to go for further help, often for free.

Many of the rights we enjoy come from the law, and where the law in Scotland and Northern Ireland differs from that of England and Wales I have made reference to this.

I should like to acknowledge the assistance of Geoffrey Woodroffe, solicitor, and Director of the Centre for Consumer Law at Brunel University, who read the manuscript and made many helpful suggestions.

When I started writing I had in mind a book which would find its way on to the kitchen shelf, along with all the indispensable cookbooks, or on to the telephone table, along with the telephone directory and other vital books of information. But wherever you decide to keep it I hope readers will find it helpful.

Gaynor Morgan
May 1988

A

ABTA

The Association of British Travel Agents is the trade association of the travel industry. Ninety per cent of tour operators and travel agents are members. If you have a problem with a package holiday, the hotel was overbooked, a promised sea view was only visible by telescope, and you don't get a satisfactory answer from your tour operator, ABTA may be able to help. They will look into the problem and, if they think you have a good case, can ask the tour operator to reconsider. They can intervene in disputes with travel agents too.

ABTA can only deal with disputes involving tour operators or travel agents who are members. So, check for the ABTA sign at the back of the brochure or in the agent's window. They can't deal with claims for illness or injury and any claim must be made within nine months of returning from the holiday concerned. Of the disputes ABTA are asked to conciliate, about half not put to the tour operator because ABTA believes the holidaymaker does not have a valid case, and even if they do think you have a good case they can't force the tour operator to pay compensation.

If conciliation fails ABTA also has an arbitration scheme which is a cheap and simple method of settling a dispute. But to use it your claim

must be against an ABTA tour operator and not a travel agent, and both sides must agree to abide by the decision of the arbitrator, who is independent, not connected with the travel trade. Think carefully before going to arbitration because once you've done this you can't then go to court and, based on past decisions, courts are likely to make higher compensation awards than the arbitrator.

ABTA has a code of practice for travel agents and operators, breach of which can lead to fines or even expulsion from membership. It includes rules on accuracy of brochures, surcharges, holiday changes and the like. Booking through an ABTA member also gives you protection if the holiday firm goes bust.

ABTA's address is 55–57 Newman Street, London W1P 4AH, 01-637 2444. The Office of Fair Trading also produces a free leaflet on package holidays and the ABTA Code is available from Citizens Advice Bureaux and consumer advice centres.

See also: ATOL, BROCHURES, HOLIDAYS

ACAS

The Advisory, Conciliation and Arbitration Service is an independent body, set up by statute, which helps with and advises on employment problems. There are branches around Britain which deal with hundreds of queries and requests for advice each week.

ACAS has officers who are trained to conciliate or mediate in disputes between employers and employees, on an informal basis. For example, if an employee has been dismissed, an ACAS conciliation officer may assist the parties in trying to settle a claim for unfair dismissal either before a formal complaint has been made to an industrial tribunal or once the complaint has been lodged.

Its arbitration services are most commonly used in disputes between unions and management, and although any recommendations ACAS makes are not legally binding, because arbitration has been chosen by both parties, they usually accept the outcome.

ACAS also has a code of practice on employment to which all employers should adhere. If they don't, this breach can be used at an industrial tribunal hearing to show that an employer has behaved unreasonably.

ACAS head office is at 11–12 St James's Square, London SW1Y 4LA, 01-210 3600, plus regional offices.

See also: ARBITRATION

Accountants

There is no need to have any formal training to call yourself an accountant, so before you use one it's best to check that he or she is qualified. The initials to look for after their name are FCA, ACA, FCCA, or ACCA. The former two show that he or she is a chartered accountant and has passed the exams set by the Institute of Chartered Accountants in England and Wales (sister bodies for Scotland and Northern Ireland), the latter two indicate certified accountants who have passed exams set by the Chartered Association of Certified Accountants. The Institute of Chartered Accountants' address is Chartered Accountants Hall, PO Box 433, 1 Moorgate Place, London EC2P 2BJ, 01-628 7060, and in Scotland, 27 Queen Street, Edinburgh EH2 1LA, 031-225 5673. The Chartered Association of Certified Accountants' address is 29 Lincoln's Inn Fields, London WC2A 3EE, 01-242 6855. Both organisations have lists of qualified accountants and will look into complaints against their members including claims of bad service or allegations of misconduct. They will not enter into disputes about bills and cannot award compensation; for this you would have to go to court.

As with any other service, ask about charges before employing an accountant. They may not be able to give you an exact price but should be able to give you examples of charges for you to compare with other firms. Accountants will advise on a whole range of financial services but most people who consult them do so over tax matters. Unless you have complicated tax returns to do then ask yourself whether you really need to go to the expense of employing an accountant. The Inland Revenue's own PAYE enquiry offices can be very helpful on tax matters, and their service is free. To find your nearest office look in the phone book under Inland Revenue.

See also: TAX

Advance Payments

Advance payments or deposits are what you might be asked to pay to secure services or goods which may have to be ordered or made for you. They are goodwill payments, to show that you genuinely intend to buy, and are usually non-returnable if you subsequently break the agreement by cancelling the order, though some shops will let you off. The general rule is never to hand over a full payment in advance. If you pay a deposit make sure you get a written receipt showing how much you paid and giving the name and address of the firm or shop. But there is still a danger that if the supplier goes bust, your money will be lost.

You will be able to demand your deposit back if the seller breaks the contract. If, for example, the goods are not delivered on time or if the goods turn out to be faulty.

You may be asked to pay something in advance for services such as building work to cover the cost of materials. Be wary of this, large and reputable firms rarely ask it. But if you do decide to pay only hand over what you consider to be a reasonable amount to cover the cost of materials.

It is quite common to have to pay the full amount in advance if you are buying goods through a mail order advertisement.

See also: CONSUMER CREDIT ACT, CREDIT, MAIL ORDER

Advertising

Legal, decent, honest and truthful – that's the rule advertisements are meant to follow. For some products there are special codes, for example, ads for alcohol should not be directed at young people, nor should they give the impression that drink can lead to sexual success, and cigarette ads have to be approved before publication. These days most adverts are pretty truthful but still a few misleading ones slip through the net. If you want to complain about an ad in a newspaper, magazine or on a poster contact the Advertising Standards Authority (ASA), Brook House, 2–16 Torrington Place, London WC1E 7HN, 01-580 5555. The ASA is an independent watchdog, paid for by a surcharge on most ads (but not TV or radio advertising). They operate the British Code of Advertising Practice which gives guidance on what can and cannot be said in an advert. The ASA receives more than 7,000 complaints each year and can make the advertiser amend or withdraw the ad or ask the publication in which the ad appeared not to publish it again.

For ads on television or radio the Independent Broadcasting Authority, 70 Brompton Road, London SW3 1EY, 01-584 7011 is the body to moan to. Believe it or not the IBA rejects about 20 per cent of all advertisements submitted for transmission.

If you think an advertiser is guilty of misrepresentation, a criminal offence, report it to your local trading standards or consumer protection department, who may decide to prosecute. In such cases you may be able to claim compensation.

See also: BARGAINS, BROADCASTING, MAIL ORDER (for Direct Mail advertising), MISLEADING PRICES

Advice and Assistance Scheme
See: GREEN FORM SCHEME

Association of British Travel Agents
See: ABTA

After Sales Service
One of the key questions to ask when you buy anything which could go wrong, be it a television, a car or a washing machine, is 'What about the after sales service?' The shop itself may offer a repair service or the manufacturer may offer a guarantee. Some insurance schemes are available, at a price, which cover breakdown of the goods for a certain period. Check all this before you buy. The cost of after sales service can make a considerable difference to the price you pay for the goods. For example, a £320 washing machine with a four-year guarantee is probably a better deal than one at £270 with only a one-year guarantee.

But don't forget that if the goods go wrong within a reasonable time, usually a few weeks after purchase, then under the Sale of Goods Act, you may have a right to a full refund from the shop where you bought them anyway. And as the goods must be reasonably durable, you may be able to claim compensation for the cost of repairs even years after the original purchase, depending on the price you paid and the seriousness of the defect. Why? The guarantee is additional to your statutory rights against the shop.

See also: GUARANTEES, MAINTENANCE CONTRACTS, MERCHANTABLE QUALITY, SALE OF GOODS ACT, WARRANTY

Air Travel
Travelling to and from your holiday destination can be a trying time beset with problems. According to Actionwoman's annual holiday survey, delays at airports, overbooking of aircraft seats and your baggage taking a trip to Ibiza while you fly to Crete are the most common.

DELAYS: There is no cast-iron guarantee you'll depart and arrive at the scheduled time – the small print on the ticket usually carries a disclaimer to this effect. So, if you miss a multi-million pound deal because your flight is late it's just your bad luck. While you can't expect compensation for delays caused by a strike, poor weather conditions or anything outside the control of the airline, you may be able to get some money

back if you can prove that the airline could have avoided the delay but, a word of warning, it'll be a struggle.

If your delay is a long one the airline will probably provide you with a free meal and, if it's overnight and practicable, hotel accommodation. If they don't, then get together with other stranded passengers and complain, on the spot, to the airline representative. Also check your holiday insurance. Most policies cover airport delays of over a certain duration and you can now sometimes take out delay compensation insurance for an extra premium.

OVERBOOKING: On scheduled flights as many as 25 per cent of passengers who have booked seats will not claim them. Business travellers who can't be sure when they'll need to fly and passengers who miss connections are among those who become 'no shows'. To compensate for this airlines overbook flights and usually they get their sums right; but occasionally they don't and then have to 'bump' passengers off the flight. In the US this has become a profitable sideline for some travellers who volunteer to be 'bumped' in return for a compensation payment and then keep their ticket to fly at a later time. In Britain it is usually the last people to check in who are 'bumped' but it may not be long before we follow the US in giving people the option, which is, after all, a fairer system and one which keeps most passengers happy. If it happens to you and you are delayed, you may be entitled to compensation from the airline.

BAGGAGE: You've arrived at your holiday hot spot. You've watched everyone else's cases sail round the carousel only to find yours have gone on a holiday all on their own in the opposite direction. Don't panic.

If your luggage does not turn up report it to a representative at the airline desk or speak immediately to your holiday rep. If you can't find either, report the missing luggage at the airport's lost and found office and make sure you get a note from them showing you've reported the loss. Make sure you also have the baggage tags which should have been attached to your airline ticket when you checked in on departure. These will help you in your claim for compensation.

If you need to buy essential items, while you wait for the missing luggage to reappear, then ask the airline for money. If they refuse buy the items but keep receipts to claim from the airline when you get home. You should claim baggage compensation within 21 days of its loss – if it doesn't turn up. How much you get depends on the weight of the bag and contents rather than the price you paid.

If luggage is damaged in transit or something is missing, to claim compensation go to the airline or handling agent's desk at the airport and report the fact immediately. If you don't notice straight away you should report it within seven days. However, you'd probably be better off claiming through your holiday insurance, if you can, as you may get a higher payment.

Airlines are usually helpful but if you're not satisfied with their response to your complaint you should write to the Air Transport Users' Committee, 129 Kingsway, London WC2B 6NN, 01-242 3882, who can investigate for you. For complaints about airports write to the individual airport or for Heathrow, Gatwick, Stanstead, Prestwick, Aberdeen, Edinburgh and Glasgow airports, to the Airport Consultative Committee, British Airports Authority, 130 Wilton Road, London SW1.

See also: ABTA, ATOL, BUCKET SHOPS, HOLIDAY INSURANCE, HOLIDAYS, TRAVEL AGENTS, TRAVELLERS' CHEQUES

Air Travel Organiser's Licence
See: ATOL

Animals
What happens if your dog or cat strays and causes injury to a neighbour or damages his property? Generally, you are only liable, and will have to pay compensation for the damage, if you have been negligent. Whether you are negligent depends on whether you have taken reasonable steps to avoid it happening. So, if your dog strays into the road and causes an accident you could not be held liable if you left it enclosed in your garden

and it escaped because a visitor left the garden gate open. It could then be argued that you had done all that could be reasonably expected of you to prevent the dog's escaping. If, on the other hand, you let it out of the front door for a walk on its own you could be liable. If the animal is known to be dangerous, such as a dog with rabies or a particularly temperamental horse, or is of a dangerous species such as a lion, then you can be liable for the damage caused even though you were not negligent. Similarly with livestock. So watch out if your pet goat wanders next door and 'prunes' the neighbours' herbaceous border.

APR
See: CREDIT

Arbitration
Arbitration is a method of settling a dispute without a formal court hearing. Both parties agree to an independent person, an arbitrator (arbiter in Scotland), looking at all the evidence, considering the relevant law and resolving the matter. If you decide to use arbitration the decision is usually binding on both parties. Usually you cannot appeal or choose to go to court later, if you do not like the outcome.

Some disputes have to be settled by arbitration because it is stipulated in a previous agreement. For example some furniture removal firms put this in their contract and, once agreed to, you lose the right to take a dispute to court unless the firm agrees. This is not a desirable situation for the consumer as it reduces your rights considerably, and though it doesn't necessarily mean that you will lose out, in practice arbitrators generally make lower compensation awards than courts.

If a trader is a member of a trade association they may have a code of practice which includes an arbitration scheme. ABTA, for example, has such a scheme to help settle complaints about member package tour operators. The use of such schemes is optional. They are cheap, but not free.

As we have said before, you can sometimes get a better deal by going to court, so you should weigh up the advantages and disadvantages of each method before agreeing to anything. Arbitration is generally decided on written evidence so if you feel that your case would be better presented in person or it is very complicated you might prefer to go to court. On the other hand, if you'd prefer not to appear arbitration may be the answer. Also under arbitration there are no massive costs to pay if you lose, and if a trade association is involved they can put pressure on a trader to pay up. It is not an easy decision and it is best to seek legal advice if you have a choice open to you or ask your Citizens Advice Bureau for guidance.

See also: ACAS, CODES OF PRACTICE, OMBUDSMEN, SMALL CLAIMS, TRADE ASSOCIATIONS

Architects

To call yourself an architect you must be registered with the Architects Registration Council of the United Kingdom (ARCUK), and it is an offence for anyone to call themselves an architect unless they are qualified and registered under the Architects Registration Act.

If you have a complaint against an architect first give him or her the chance to put it right. If this fails you have a choice of courses to take. First, you could pursue your rights under the Supply of Goods and Services Act 1982. When you employ an architect you enter a legally binding contract, and the price charged, the standard of work carried out and the time taken must all be reasonable. If they are not, or the architect is in breach of any other part of the contract, you can pursue a claim for compensation through the courts.

The majority of architects, around 90 per cent, are members of their professional body, The Royal Institute of British Architects (RIBA) or sister bodies in Scotland and Northern Ireland. Their members are subject to a code of professional conduct and RIBA will fully investigate any complaint involving a breach of that code. They can take disciplinary action against members, if necessary, but cannot insist that an architect pays compensation. They will also have lists of local architects doing the kind of work you have in mind. The Royal Incorporation of Architects in Scotland and the Royal Society of Ulster Architects will investigate complaints against their members in Scotland and Northern Ireland.

In cases of 'disgraceful conduct' ARCUK will investigate a complaint and can actually strike an architect off the register.

As with all contracts for services check the details before signing. If you have a complaint try to sort it out with the architect first. If you are in doubt about how to complain or who to complain to, RIBA or its Scottish or Ulster equivalent can advise you.

USEFUL ADDRESSES:

Architects Registration Council of the United Kingdom, 73 Hallam Street, London W1N 6EE, 01-580 5861

Royal Incorporation of Architects in Scotland,
15 Rutland Square, Edinburgh EH1 2BE, 031-229 7205

Royal Society of Ulster Architects,
2 Mount Charles, Belfast BT7 1NZ, (0232) 323760

Royal Institute of British Architects,
66 Portland Place, London W1N 4AD, 01-580 5533

See also: SERVICES

ATOL

Anyone who offers travel to the public using seats on a charter air flight
must have an Air Travel Organiser's Licence (ATOL) from the Civil
Aviation Authority. The operator pays a sum of money into a central
fund to cover the cost of getting holidaymakers home, and refunds for
people who have paid but not yet been on their holiday, should the
travel organiser go bust. Look for the ATOL symbol in holiday
brochures. For further information on ATOL write to CAA, ATOL
section, 45 Kingsway, London WC2B 6TE, 01-379 7311.

See also: ABTA, AIR TRAVEL, HOLIDAY INSURANCE, HOLIDAYS

Auctions

Auctions are the ideal place to find unusual items from furniture in need
of renovation to priceless artefacts. Your purchase may be more modest
than a million-pound Van Gogh but it still pays to know your rights.

Usually auctions are held at an auctioneer's salerooms or, in the case
of a house clearance, for example, they could be held in the house in
question. Generally sales notices at the place of sale or in the local paper
give the date of the sale and times for viewing, when the goods will be
displayed for would-be buyers to inspect them. Be warned, viewing
could be *just* before the sale starts.

If you buy at auction you do so at your own risk. The Sale of Goods
rights which cover most other forms of purchasing don't usually apply.
Most auctioneers impose conditions of sale which in effect take away
your legal rights, provided they are reasonable. Look for them pinned
up in the auction room or listed in the catalogue. Usually they say
that you buy at your own risk. It is up to you to inspect an item *before*
bidding for it. It is also likely that the conditions of sale give auctioneers
and previous owners a let out if the item doesn't turn out to be exactly as

described. Look for clauses like 'Every lot is sold with all faults and errors of description.' Catalogue and oral descriptions are, however, covered by the Trade Descriptions Act although few prosecutions have been brought. In most cases descriptions give very few details and, as far as they go, tend to be accurate.

Some items, or 'lots', have a reserve price on them. This is a price below which the auctioneer will not sell. Once you've bid successfully you either have to pay a substantial deposit – 25 per cent is not uncommon – and the balance within a couple of days or all the money immediately. It is your duty to organise delivery of the goods and to make sure they're insured immediately – if they are valuable.

Buying at auction is risky but it's also fun and you can pick up some real bargains. Just remember two golden rules, examine the goods closely *before* you bid and check the small print on the Conditions of Sale.

See also: DISCLAIMERS, DUTCH AUCTIONS, MOCK AUCTIONS

B

Bank Charges

Staying in the black is the key to happy banking. If you don't, you can expect to pay hefty bank charges on every transaction from cashing cheques to paying direct debits, and that is just throwing money away. Banks estimate that one in three of their customers pays charges because their accounts go into the red from time to time. Even if you just slip into the red once you will probably be liable for charges for the whole charging period, which can be as long as three months. It's worth checking with your bank how their charging periods run and to plan ahead, trying to get into the black before the new period starts.

Banks have different charges for different things but some are better than others at explaining them on your statement.

Here are just some of the charges that might be added to your bill if you overdraw . . .

· a charge for going overdrawn without arrangement.
· the cost of warning letters telling you you are overdrawn.
· a charge for bouncing a cheque.
· an overdraft arrangement fee for putting the imbalance on an agreed footing.
· interest on the amount you are overdrawn.
· the cost of each debit – cheque, standing order, direct debit and cash dispenser withdrawal.

Some banks waive charges if they are under a certain amount, others make a notional interest allowance for the money you have had in your account while it was in credit during that charging period. If you go into the red only very occasionally, yet still get stung by charges, you could write to your manager. Individual managers may be able to waive charges or amend them if they think it appropriate. Some banks may take your average balance for the quarter into account, for example, if you usually have £500 in your account and have only overdrawn once during the period they may decide to waive or amend the charges.

If you regularly fall into the red you can easily end up paying as much as £100 a year in charges so, if staying in the black is impossible, try cutting down on the number of transactions the bank undertakes for you. For example, use your credit card and pay that off each month with just one cheque.

See also: BANKS

Bankruptcy

In the scramble that follows when a business goes bust ordinary customers are usually the last to get their money back. More than 20,000 companies crash each year, and when it comes to dividing up any assets that are left banks, the Inland Revenue and local authorities, for rate arrears, are just a few of the institutions who have priority in the pay out.

We are most at risk when we pay in advance for goods or services, for example for airline tickets, goods bought by mail order and major household items from double glazing to fitted kitchens. The chances of getting money back, or even part of it, may be slim but it's still worth a try. If you are the victim of a failed firm then check with your local paper – lists of bankruptcies and liquidations are generally published there. You should then write to the named liquidator and make sure that your claim is registered with him. Then when all the inquiries have been made and priority claimants paid, if there are any funds left at the end of the day you will get your money back or at least a percentage of it.

There is no truth in the well worn statement 'I was made bankrupt overnight'. It can take months to go through all the legal formalities, during which time attempts are made to save the business and creditors have a chance to stake their claim. This is what is happening when you read that a company has 'gone into liquidation'. In fact, companies don't actually go bankrupt, only individuals can be declared bankrupt.

A central register of bankrupts is kept at the Law Courts, Strand, London WC2 which anyone can inspect for a few pence. You must, however, go there in person: information will not be given over the phone.

We cannot be expected to know all the facts we need to safeguard our money when we enter a contract with a trader, but there are a few things we can do to help avoid being the victim of a company's financial failure. Avoid paying in advance: offer to pay in instalments or ask for credit terms. Better still pay with your credit card. If the transaction is over £100 you may then be able to claim against the finance company as well, under the Consumer Credit Act. Ask for a financial reference for the trader. Ask whether money is protected if their company fails, for example do they keep customers' deposits in a separate bank account? Ask whether there's a trade federation covering the particular work or service. If the trader is a member he may be paying into an indemnity scheme which ensures that the job would still be carried out if he went bust.

See also: ADVANCE PAYMENTS, CONSUMER CREDIT ACT, MAIL ORDER

Banks

Whether or not you're happy with your bank the fact is that around 30 million of us have bank current accounts and 90 per cent of customers stay with the same bank most of their lives. As with other services, when you open a bank account you make a contract with your bank and therefore there are certain rights and duties that exist between you.

The bank should . . .
· not bounce a cheque you have written so long as you have funds in your account or an overdraft agreement to cover it. If they wrongly bounce one you could in fact sue for damage to your reputation.
· not bounce a cheque, even if you don't have money in your account, if it is backed by a cheque card.
· give you competent financial advice or carry out competently probate or accountancy work for you. If you think they have been negligent you can sue.

In return you should . . .
· notify your bank of a possible fraud immediately. For example, if you have your cheque book and cheque card stolen. If you do this your account can't be debited; if you don't you could be held responsible. Banks tend to frown on people keeping their cheques and cheque

cards in the same place as stealing both makes it so much easier for a thief to draw money on them.
· keep your account in the black or agree an overdraft limit. Some banks are quite happy to allow you a regular overdraft but remember that you'll not only have to pay interest on it but will also incur bank charges. Most major banks now have special facilities for permanent overdrafts.
· keep your bank manager informed about any changes in your circumstances that could result in a shortfall in your account. Most branch managers respond well to requests for money if you tell them what's going on.

If you have a problem with your bank the Banking Ombudsman might be able to help. Funded by the major banks, he is nonetheless independent of them and can look into disputes arising since 1 January 1986 that involve the major clearing banks or their associate companies, for example Barclays Bank or Barclays Bank Trust Company. You must get in touch with the Ombudsman within six months of your last contact with the bank's office, your claim must be for less than £100,000 and the Ombudsman can't investigate if your claim is being or has been dealt with by a court.

Before resorting to the Ombudsman you should pursue your complaint first with the bank up to head office level. He cannot look into matters of bank policy nor into decisions about whether or not to provide loans or similar credit facilities unless a decision to refuse credit has been based on incorrect information held by the bank. Nor can the Ombudsman look at the way a bank has used its discretion under a will or trust.

For more detailed information about which banks are in the scheme and whether he can help you, write to the Office of the Banking Ombudsman, Citadel House, 5/11 Fetter Lane, London EC4A 1BR.

For more general information on banks and banking, contact the Banking Information Service, 10 Lombard Street, London EC3V 9AP, 01-626 8486.

See also: BANK CHARGES, BORROWING, INTEREST RATES

Bargains

There's nothing so designed to set a dedicated shopper's pulse racing than the sight of a bargain. But what is a bargain? How many of those

tempting knockdown prices can you really believe? The answer is not many. The aim of the 1987 Consumer Protection Act is to tighten up the law on price comparisons, making it an offence to give a misleading price for goods, services, accommodation or facilities (these are already covered by the Trade Descriptions Act). The Act is to be backed up by a code of practice which will give clear indications to traders about what they can and cannot say. The new legislation is an attempt to close the many loopholes which in the past have allowed traders to mislead consumers into thinking that they were saving money. Among the signs which have been allowed but which have little or no meaning are those saying 'special offer' which don't mention a higher price, 'closing down sales' which go on for months, 'introductory offers' where you're told the price will rise after a certain date and comparisons between the price of ready assembled and self assembly furniture when you can't actually buy the former in the shop. All of these are likely to come under the spotlight in the new code.

Vague price claims suggesting the goods are worth more than the price they're asking, for example 'worth £10, our price £5' are already banned, but notices such as 'was £100, now £75' are allowed so long as the item has been on sale at the higher price for 28 consecutive days during the last six months at that shop or one of its branches. The only safe bet when you see any bargain price is to compare the actual selling price with that at other shops – if it's cheaper *then* it's a bargain.

See also: SALES

Barristers

Barristers represent us in court and are instructed by solicitors. We cannot deal with them direct. If you have a complaint about the way a barrister is dealing with your case then first raise the matter with your solicitor. If this gets you nowhere, write to your barrister's head of chambers (not in Scotland or Northern Ireland where there is no chambers system). If you're still not happy then write to the General Council of the Bar, 11 South Square, Gray's Inn, London WC1R 5EL, 01-242 0082. Their professional conduct committee can investigate the case and, if appropriate, discipline the barrister. They can't award you compensation; for that you would have to sue.

Unfortunately, if your complaint is about his or her appearance in court, there's little you can do because you can't sue a barrister for negligence in their advocacy. But you could sue if you feel you've been given bad advice. Taking legal action over a barrister isn't easy so seek independent legal advice first.

Scotland and Northern Ireland have separate bodies. Make your complaint to The Faculty of Advocates in Scotland, Parliament House, Edinburgh EH1 1RF, 031-226 2881, and to the Complaints Committee of the Bar Executive Council in Northern Ireland, Bar Library, Royal Courts of Justice, Belfast BT1 3JF.

BEAB

See: COOKERS

Benefits

Every year there is a money mountain made up of unclaimed benefits as many of us fail to claim that to which we are entitled. Some benefits are based on national insurance contributions, others are non-contributory, some means-tested and some not.

The main contributory benefits are unemployment benefit, maternity allowance, retirement pension and widow's allowance. For a full list of all national insurance benefits including who's entitled, what you pay and what you get, ask at your local social security office (under Health and Social Security, Department of, in the phone book), or write to DHSS Leaflets Unit, PO Box 21, Stanmore, Middlesex HA7 1AY, or ring a government telephone advice service by dialling the DHSS Freefone 0800 666 555.

The Social Security Act 1986, which came into force in April 1988, has radically altered non-contributory benefit payments to people on low incomes. Since April 1988 supplementary benefit has been replaced by Income Support and Family Income Supplement by Family Credit. A Social Fund provides loans instead of the old system of extra single payments and special needs payments. These loans are repayable from your weekly benefit. For how this could affect you and for more details on each scheme, contact your local DHSS.

Dealing with the DHSS can be a frustrating business. Here are a few tips to help you:

· Telephoning: Who deals with your case depends on your surname, so ask for the section which deals with the benefit you're enquiring about and give the first letter of your surname. If the matter is complicated and you're not getting very far, you could ask to speak to the supervisor. If necessary, follow up your phone call with a letter and keep a copy.

· Writing: Setting things down in a letter can often bring more action than a phone call. Quote on the top any reference number you have and keep a copy. If they don't reply, phone and ask why.

· Keep all letters, assessment forms and so on from the DHSS. It makes sorting out problems or mistakes a lot easier.

If you think you are not getting as much benefit as you should, and that the DHSS has made a wrong decision, you can appeal to a social security tribunal. First you need to ask the adjudication officer dealing with your claim to look at it again. You should then get an explanation of how the decision was made. If you want to appeal to a tribunal you must write and tell your local DHSS or Employment office within three months from the date of the decision. A leaflet, *How to Appeal*, is available from your local offices.

Borrower's Rights
See: CONSUMER CREDIT ACT, HIRE PURCHASE

Borrowing
Debt is no longer a dirty word. In fact, as long as you're considered a good risk and the lender believes you will pay back, there are all sorts of people begging you to borrow money from them. You can borrow money for almost anything from paying for a holiday or buying a car to helping get over a short-term cash flow problem. But whether you want a short- or long-term loan you need to find the cheapest and most

appropriate one for you. As well as considering how much you want to borrow, and how quickly you want to pay it back, you need to compare the interest charged on various schemes. Banks, building societies, money shops, finance companies and money lenders all offer loans. For a major sum you can borrow against an insurance policy or even against your home.

HERE ARE JUST A FEW OF THE DEALS AVAILABLE:

CREDIT CARDS: Bank and store credit cards can give you up to seven weeks' interest-free credit. But don't use them for cash as you may have to pay interest straight away, or a service charge which will be a percentage of the amount you've borrowed.

OVERDRAFT: This can be one of the cheapest forms of short-term borrowing but do ask your bank manager first, otherwise, as well as annoying him, the rates could be punitive. Most arranged overdrafts set the interest rate at a few per cent over the current bank rate which generally works out lower than that of a personal bank loan. The advantage of an overdraft is that it is flexible, the quicker you pay it off the less interest you pay. The disadvantage is that you'll also become liable for bank charges and the manager can call in the outstanding amount at any time – though in practice you usually agree a time limit at the outset. Some banks now offer a permanent overdraft facility at special rates.

PERSONAL LOAN: The bank manager may prefer you to take out a personal loan rather than an overdraft so that you know exactly how much you have to pay back each month. It is more expensive than an overdraft.

SAVE AND BORROW ACCOUNTS: Sometimes called continuous credit accounts, these are offered by most banks. You pay a set amount into the account each month and are given an upper spending limit, usually a certain number of times your monthly payment. These work out expensive if you borrow a lot and only pay back the minimum each month. Choose one which pays *you* interest if you're in credit.

MONEY SHOPS: Better established in the US than here, though you can see them in the high street now. Owned by a finance company or a bank, the loans they offer are similar to those offered by the bank but the interest rate is usually higher.

MONEY LENDERS: Steer clear of these even if you're desperate! They tend to lend to people who have already been turned down by other lenders and charge very high interest rates to cover their risk.

INTEREST FREE CREDIT: The ideal way to buy household goods such as videos, washing machines, hi-fis. If you pay the full amount within a set time, which could be anything from three months to a year or more, you don't have to pay interest, though you have the advantage of paying by instalments. Check major stores for these special deals.

LOANS FROM YOUR EMPLOYER: Some larger companies offer employees loans at low interest rates or interest-free for specific things such as travel season tickets, a car or property. The main thing to consider is what happens if you leave the company.

LIFE INSURANCE POLICY: If you have a life insurance policy you may be able to borrow up to a certain amount of the cash-in value. Usually you pay the interest on the loan and the capital sum is deducted from the amount repaid to you when the policy matures.

See also: BANK CHARGES, BRIDGING LOANS, BUDGET ACCOUNTS, CREDIT, CREDIT CARDS, CREDIT UNIONS, FINANCE COMPANIES, HIRE PURCHASE, INTEREST RATES, MAIL ORDER, MORTGAGES

Brand Names

The use of brand names is very important in the marketing of most goods from cars to baked beans. A customer's loyalty to a brand is fought for in advertising campaigns and slogans such as 'Beanz Meanz Heinz'.

Legally, manufacturers can pick any name they like for a product so long as the name isn't misleading, can't be confused with another product of a same or similar name and doesn't cause offence. If a brand name is registered as a trademark then it has to satisfy certain other criteria: namely it mustn't claim the product is used by the royal family when it isn't or carry any particular meaning. For example, you couldn't register 'Good and Healthy' as a trademark because it implies that the product has those characteristics.

More often than not the trademark is just the name of the manufacturer. A few brand names that were once trademarks have now passed into common usage to describe that type of product generally, for example Linoleum; a few others are misused in this way but are still carefully protected trademarks, such as Sellotape and Hoover.

If you're sold something as a particular brand and it isn't, you can claim your money back under the Sale of Goods Act as the goods are not as described. The shopkeeper may also have committed an offence and you could report him to your local trading standards department or consumer protection office.

See also: SALE OF GOODS ACT, TRADEMARKS

Bridging Loans

Most banks offer bridging loans to bridge the gap between receiving the money from the sale of your previous home and buying your new house. It is usually for a short period and the bank will need to be satisfied that the sale of your old house will go ahead so that you can pay off the loan. Bridging loans are expensive because you are usually borrowing large sums of money.

British Standards Institution

The British Standards Institution (BSI) is an independent organisation which draws up quality and safety standards for consumer and industrial products. The first standard was in 1903 for rolled steel sections used in railway lines and there are now more than 9,000 standards. Most of them are voluntary though some are required by law, for example car seat belts. You can recognise products made to a British Standard by the relevant BS number; for example, 13 amp plugs are stamped BS 1363 as the manufacturer's claim of compliance with the standard. If a product carries the BSI kitemark, even better, because it shows that it has been independently tested to the standard by the BSI. Similarly, look for the BSI Safety Mark which denotes independent testing to the appropriate safety standard.

Kitemark   Safety Mark

If you buy something which claims to be made to the British Standard and you don't think that it is, you can complain to the BSI's certification and assessment department, BSI, Maylands Avenue, Hemel Hempstead, Hertfordshire HP2 4SU, (0442) 230442. They can then test the product and, if they agree with you, help you in your claim against the manufacturer. For further information on the role of the BSI write to BSI, 2 Park Street, London W1A 2BS.

Broadcasting

If you're outraged by the latest American comedy or horrified by the bad language in the latest soap opera then you don't have to sit in silence, you can complain to the television company showing it. If you want to complain about a BBC television or radio programme, ring 01-743 8000 and ask for the duty officer who will register your comments. For programmes shown on independent television, phone or write to the company in your area, for example Yorkshire Television, Central and so on. Most companies have special phone lines or departments to record and deal with complaints and do take them quite seriously.

The Broadcasting Complaints Commission, set up in 1981, can also consider complaints made about radio or TV programmes, adverts and teletext transmissions. Their scope, however, is very limited and for them to investigate it your complaint must be about either of the following: unjust or unfair treatment, for example, when you've taken part in a programme; unwarranted infringement of privacy, whether actually in a programme or referring to the way the material for the programme was obtained.

The Commission can't look into the quality of content or a programme in general, nor can it get involved in a complaint which might go to court. If the Commission takes up your case all you can hope is for the offending broadcasting company to publish the decision in the national press. You won't get compensation. The address of The Broadcasting Complaints Commission is Grosvenor Gardens House, 35–37 Grosvenor Gardens, London SW1W 0BS, 01-630 1966.

The BBC is financed by the licence fee and the Government, and is regulated by a Board of Governors, while independent television and radio are financed primarily by advertising revenue and are responsible to the Independent Broadcasting Authority (IBA). The individual companies nationwide consult the IBA about their programme planning and advertisements.

Independent television and radio advertising is regulated by the Independent Broadcasting Act, which sets out, among other things, a ratio of advertising to programmes. The IBA also operates a code of advertising practice which sets out what can and can't be said in adverts and protects us against misleading ads. It was through the code that cigarette advertisements were banned on television.

If you think an advert you have seen or heard is misleading or want to complain about it in any way, write to the Independent Broadcasting Authority, 70 Brompton Road, London SW3 1EY saying when and where you saw or heard the advert and explaining your complaint. Although thousands of television and radio adverts are broadcast each year only a few hundred complaints are upheld following an IBA inquiry – a reflection of the rigorous standards imposed on advertisements in Britain.

See also: ADVERTISING

Brochures

When you book your annual holiday each year often all you really have to go on is what the glossy brochure tells you about the resort and the holiday. But just how accurate do they have to be? For example, if you're promised an Olympic-size swimming pool or a sea view what can you do if this isn't true?

If something is described in a holiday brochure and the description turns out to be false, then you can sue for breach of contract. However, many holiday companies put let-out or exclusion clauses in the small print of the booking conditions. They say things like 'We cannot be held responsible if some of the facilities in this brochure are not available owing to maintenance or cleaning work', which virtually means don't blame us if you can't use the pool. Whether or not these clauses are legal depends on whether or not they are reasonable. ABTA, the tour operators' trade association, has drawn up a code which says brochures should be clear and accurate, and that includes prices. Holiday companies don't like to pay out compensation but will usually eventually offer you some money back if you have a good case and you persist. If you think something is misdescribed, then the company may have committed an offence under the Trade Descriptions Act and you should tell your local trading standards or consumer protection officer.

See also: ABTA, EXCLUSION CLAUSES, HOLIDAYS

Brokers

A broker, whether of insurance, credit or stocks and shares, is a person licensed to sell, usually acting as an agent or middleman between the customer and the seller. Some brokers don't charge the customer for their services but receive commission from the person whose services or products they are selling, for example insurance brokers. Others, like stockbrokers, take a percentage of the transaction they arrange for you.

Since the Financial Services Act 1986 brokers have to take reasonable steps to seek out and recommend what they believe to be the best product on the market to suit your needs. They should offer independent advice and they must tell you if they charge a commission. Insurance brokers must be registered with their professional body, the Insurance Brokers Registration Council. They have a code of conduct which imposes certain rules on their members and can look into complaints against members and de-register them if necessary. Their address is 15 St Helen's Place, London EC3A 6DS, 01-588 4387.

Credit brokers are anyone who introduces customers to sources of credit. They too must be licensed and include estate agents, shops and car dealers.

See also: PAWNBROKERS, STOCKBROKERS

BSI

See BRITISH STANDARDS INSTITUTION

Bucket Shops

Buying an airline ticket through a bucket shop can cut as much as two-thirds off the cost of a flight. It is not illegal to buy from one (though selling through one is!) and as long as you exercise some caution when booking, your money should be safe.

Bucket shops are agencies which sell airline tickets at well below the official airline price. Airline fares are decided by the Government and the airlines and depend a lot on the cost of fuel, and for an airline to sell below this official price is illegal. But every year more seats are available on aircraft than are sold at the normal economy rate. In 1982, for example, 775 million seats were available and only 479 million were sold at the full fare. So for the airlines it becomes a matter of selling the seats at any price they can get – and they turn, unofficially, to bucket shops.

Bucket shops get their name from past sharp practices on the stock

market where unlicensed brokers sold worthless shares by the bucket
load. Not surprisingly they would prefer to be dubbed discount ticket
agencies! There are currently about 1,000 in Britain. A tacit agreement
with the airlines, who don't want the sale of full fares affected, means
they keep a low profile, put discreet ads in national papers and travel
magazines and operate from back rooms rather than prime high street
locations.

If you want to buy from a bucket shop first check the price of the
official fare with airlines. Ask the bucket shop which airline the flight
will be with, whether you will have to change flights, particularly with
long haul flights, whether there are any restrictions such as minimum
stay requirements and what happens if you want to change the booking
or cancel altogether. There have been a few problems with bucket shops
but, as with any advance booking, try to pay only a deposit at first and
pay this in person so you can check out what sort of organisation you are
dealing with. Also it might be worth a quick call to the airline in question
to make sure they have your reservation.

See also: AIR TRAVEL, HOLIDAYS

Budget Accounts

A special account offered by some banks to help spread the cost of
regular household bills. You add up all your expected bills for the
coming year, divide by twelve and then pay into the account that
amount each month drawing on it to meet the bills when they come in.
You usually have a separate cheque book for this account. The bank will
honour cheques paid out as long as you keep paying in. There is a charge
for a budget account service. It would be cheaper to work out your own
budget and pay that amount into a building society account each month
where it will earn you interest until you need it.

See also: BORROWING (Save and Borrow Accounts)

Builders

How do you find a good builder when you want one? Surprisingly,
perhaps, according to a *Which?* report in 1985, most of us do find one.
Which? asked 400 members of the Consumers' Association who had
recently used a builder's services if they were satisfied with the work
they'd had done and the majority said that they were.

If you're thinking of making any major structural changes to your
property first check whether you need planning permission with your

local planning department at the Town Hall or District Offices. They may be able to help you decide exactly what needs doing. Then find a builder. If no friend or family member can recommend one, choose one who is a member of a trade association. Preferably ask two or three different builders to give you a price for the job and compare them. In law, if a builder gives you a quotation, then the price is binding; if he only gives you an estimate it's not. So check which he's giving you and ask him to put in writing what you are getting for your money and when the job will start and end. And remember, even if it's only an estimate, if the final bill is too high you need only pay what is reasonable for the job. If the work is going to cost thousands, it would be quite reasonable to ask to see some of the builder's previous work before employing him. Any work carried out by a builder is covered by the Supply of Goods and Services Act (see SERVICES).

If you deal with a builder who is a member of a trade association you should be better protected. Many have guarantee schemes which act as a backup for the consumer. For example, the Building Employers' Confederation, 82 New Cavendish Street, London W1M 8AD will do the following if one of their members lets you down: put right any defects

within a certain time or finish the job satisfactorily if, for example, the member goes bust.

Other associations which can help you find a reputable builder are the Federation of Master Builders, 33 John Street, London WC1N 2BB and the Scottish Building Employers' Federation, 13 Woodside Crescent, Glasgow G3 7UP.

If you buy new property under 10 years old or are having a house built, make sure it is covered by a National House Building Council (NHBC) certificate. This means that the builder is on the NHBC register and that the property conforms to their standards. If it does, it will be issued with a certificate which gives you some protection should certain faults appear during the first 10 years after construction. It doesn't include all defects but does cover you if the builder goes bust. (For addresses see under NATIONAL.)

See also: ESTIMATES, PLANNING PERMISSION, SERVICES

Building Societies

In the mid 1980s building societies underwent a revolution. The Building Societies Act opened the door for our societies to not only provide a safe place for our savings and loans to buy property, but also to offer a whole range of financial services from insurance and estate agency facilities to general banking services including cheque book accounts. Building societies offer a reasonable return for your money and are very safe and shouldn't be underestimated as a valuable place for easy access savings.

They get their funds from investors, most of them investing small sums. They offer a variety of accounts with varying interest rates depending on how much you invest and for how long. For example, a 'higher interest' account pays a better rate of interest in return for your investing for longer periods. You usually have to make a higher initial deposit, £500 or more, and may have to give several months' notice of a withdrawal.

Half the adult population of Britain has a building society account so it is quite surprising that the number of complaints about them is very small. If you feel you have a genuine grouse, write to the manager of the branch concerned and explain the problem, telling him or her what you think should be done about it. He, or she, may be able to put things right. In practice building societies are usually very keen to keep their customers happy. If you're not satisfied then write to the society's head office. Your final course of action would be to write to the Building Societies Ombudsman, First Floor, Grosvenor Gardens House, 35–37 Grosvenor Gardens, London SW1X 7AW, 01-931 0044. The Ombudsman has the power to recommend awards up to £10,000.

See also: MORTGAGES

Bulk Buying

The more you buy the more you save. Well, at least that's the theory. But it's no good buying 10 kilos of carrots if you don't like carrots or have nowhere to store them! If you are thinking of buying in bulk here are a few points worth considering:

· Make the most of seasonal shopping, for example, buying fresh fruit and vegetables when prices are cheapest.
· Buy with a group of friends and divide the load between you. Sometimes you have to buy a minimum quantity which is too much for one person or a family.
· Shop around. Sometimes bulk prices are misleading and may not be any lower than similar goods at a large supermarket.
· Check if there are any organised bulk buying groups, sometimes called food co-ops, in your area which you could join.

If the goods turn out to be faulty your rights are the same as with any other purchase. Under the Sale of Goods Act the goods must be as described, of merchantable quality and fit for their purpose. If you're buying in bulk after selecting from a sample then the bulk must be of the same or similar quality as the sample.

See also: SALE OF GOODS ACT

Buses and Coaches

Britain's 70,000 buses and coaches shift the equivalent of the world's total population every eight months and each of us makes an average of 113 journeys a year. The Department of Transport carries out stringent safety checks on all vehicles and their drivers have to hold a public service vehicle driving licence. Most bus companies, private and public, and two-thirds of all coach operators are members of the Bus and Coach Council, Sardinia House, 52 Lincoln's Inn Fields, London WC2. The Council will consider serious complaints, for example about safety, against members. They also have a code of conduct to which members should adhere.

See also: TRANSPORT

C

CAB
See: CITIZENS ADVICE BUREAUX

CACs
See: CONSUMER ADVICE CENTRES

Caravan Repairs
See: VEHICLE BUILDERS AND REPAIRERS ASSOCIATION

Carpets
The main problems with carpets are late delivery and poor wear. As with all goods, when you buy a carpet you are covered by the Sale of Goods Act if it turns out to be faulty. However, proving that it hasn't worn well because it is defective is not always easy and you may have to agree to have the carpet independently tested to prove your point. When buying a carpet tell the seller where you want it for so that they can sell you the correct grade of carpet for the room. For example, you can't expect a bedroom quality carpet to wear well on the stairs. If you have to order a carpet then delivery should be within a reasonable time and if you need it within a specified time then make that a part of the contract and stress that the delivery date is important. Measuring for and fitting carpets is covered by the Supply of Goods and Services Act (SGSA).

Some carpet retailers are members of the National Association of Retail Furnishers, 17–21 George Street, Croydon CR9 1TQ. This trade association subscribes to the Furniture Code of Practice covering the sale of new carpets and will look into complaints against members. They will carry out independent examinations if your dispute is over quality and also offer arbitration as an alternative to taking your case to court.

If your complaint is against a carpet cleaning company then pursue your rights under the SGSA which says that reasonable care should be taken to do the job in reasonable time for a reasonable price.

See also: ARBITRATION, CODES OF PRACTICE, SALE OF GOODS ACT, SERVICES

Cars

In the Office of Fair Trading (OFT) league table of consumer complaints cars are always near the top of the list. They are not only costly to buy but also to repair, which makes it all the more important that you get a fair deal. The motor trade associations and OFT together have drawn up a code of practice which lays down standards members must follow and give you rights over and above your normal Sale of Goods rights. If a dealer is displaying one of the trade association's symbols shown below, he is bound by the code.

BUYING NEW: Your legal rights are the same as when you buy any other goods. Under the Sale of Goods Act the car should not be defective in any way; it should be fit for its purpose and as described. If not the dealer is breaking his contract with you and you can have your money back. In a recent case a Mr Bernstein bought a brand new Nissan car only to have it break down, with a serious defect, 100 or so miles later. A court said that as he'd had the car for a month it was too late to reject it for being faulty under the Sale of Goods Act so he could not have his money back but he was awarded compensation. Encouraged by the AA, Mr Bernstein appealed, and the matter was finally settled out of court. The motto of the Bernstein case is to go back to the dealer and tell him you reject the car as quickly as possible if a serious defect occurs. If the problem is minor it would be reasonable to accept a repair and, if appropriate, compensation, although you could reject here too if you were quick.

BUYING SECONDHAND: Generally speaking a secondhand car will not be expected to come up to the standard of a new one and you should inspect it thoroughly before handing over any money. If you suspect the clock has been turned back then tell your local trading standards or consumer protection department as this is a criminal offence. It is also a misdescription entitling you to reject the car or claim compensation.

If you buy from a dealer your normal Sale of Goods rights apply. If he draws your attention to a defect before you buy or you have the car

independently tested, then the dealer can't be held responsible for that defect or any that the inspection should have revealed. If you buy from a dealer who is a member of a trade association then you will be protected by the code of practice. It is always a good idea to have all the important facts put in writing, including the price, mileage and condition of the car.

If you buy from a private individual your rights are more limited, so be careful. They will largely depend on what is said between you at the time about the car's condition and value, as the only part of the Sale of Goods Act which applies is that the car should be as described and belong to the seller. Have a friend with you to take a note of what is said. If, for example, the seller tells you that the car has only had one owner and you find out it's had more owners than Genevieve, then you could be entitled to compensation. It is always best to have a secondhand car examined by an expert before you buy. Any local mechanic would probably oblige or one of the motoring associations, but you would have to pay of course.

Watch out for traders masquerading as private sellers by using small ads to sell their cars. There's nothing wrong with this if they admit they're traders, but some pretend to be private individuals to try to deprive you of your buyer's rights. This is a criminal offence.

If you buy a car at a motor auction you may pick up a bargain but you may pick up a heap, and if you do, you have very little protection in law (see AUCTIONS).

SELLING A CAR: Stick to the truth, avoid making extravagant claims and if you know it needs a major repair say so as it is an offence to sell a vehicle which is unroadworthy.

AT THE GARAGE: 'Thank you sir, that'll be £353.92 plus VAT.'

'But I only wanted a service.'

How can you avoid nasty shocks like that? The trouble with work on cars is that it is often difficult for the garage to know what is wrong, and therefore how much it is likely to cost to put it right, before starting work. So, unless it's something routine like a service, ask the garage not to go ahead with work over a certain sum without checking with you first. If you can get a written quotation, even better, they should then stick to that figure for the specified job. If they only give you an estimate, the final bill should still be near the estimated sum for the agreed work. If no amount is discussed, then the bill should be reasonable for the work done.

If you dispute the bill the garage might have what is called a lien on the car which means they can hold it until you pay up. In these circumstances you could: offer what you consider to be a reasonable amount and demand the car (if they don't hand it over tell them you'll sue to recover it and for compensation); pay the bill and take legal action against them to recover the disputed amount; or leave the car until the matter is settled. Unfortunately, if you take the car before the matter has been dealt with, you could be found guilty of stealing your own car!

Repairs should be carried out with reasonable skill in a reasonable time and using suitable materials. If not, then you may have a claim under the Supply of Goods and Services Act (see SERVICES).

CAR-PARKS: Don't assume, when you pay to park your car, that the car-park is under any special duty to look after it. If it's broken into, stolen or damaged they cannot usually be held responsible.

If you have a problem which can't be sorted out with the dealer and he is a member of a trade association, ask them to intervene. They will do what they can to settle the dispute. They can also refer your case to arbitration, if you agree. Before agreeing to this take legal advice because it might be better to go to court yourself and you can't do both. If the firm you're dealing with isn't a member of an association, motoring organisations like the AA or RAC may be prepared to take up your case if you're a member.

The following trade associations all subscribe to the Code of Practice for the Motor Industry, which covers sales practices for new and used cars, spare parts and accessories, as well as servicing and body and general repairs. You can write to:

The Conciliation Service, Motor Agents Association Limited (MAA), 73 Park Street, Bristol BS1 5PS for all complaints except those about new cars

Customer Complaints Service, Scottish Motor Trade Association Limited (SMTA), 3 Palmerston Place, Edinburgh EH12 5AF for all complaints in Scotland except about new cars

The Customer Relations Adviser, Society of Motor Manufacturers and Traders Limited (SMMT), Forbes House, Halkin Street, London SW1X 7DS for all new car complaints

There is also an OFT code covering vehicle body repairs which members of the Vehicle Builders and Repairers Association adhere to. Address complaints about their members' work to the Conciliation Service, VBRA, Belmont House, 102 Finkle Lane, Gildersome, Leeds LS27 7TW.

Full details on buying a car and codes of practice are contained in a free OFT leaflet available from local Citizens Advice Bureaux and consumer advice centres.

See also: ARBITRATION, AUCTIONS, SALE OF GOODS ACT, SERVICES

Cash Dispensers

Formally called automated teller machines or ATMs, just about every street corner bank plus many building societies now has one of these hole-in-the-wall automatic cash dispensers which give money at any time of day or night, weekends included. Once restricted to giving cash only, the latest models check the balance of your account, order you a new cheque book and even accept deposits.

The keys to this range of computerised banking services are a plastic card and a personal identification or 'pin' number. This is a four-figure number, usually chosen at random by computer, and known only by the customer.

But the increased use of ATMs has led to an increase in the number of possible mistakes, which occur either through machine error or fraud. For example withdrawals which have never been made appear on statements. Cash point problems head the complaints league.

If you have a problem with a cash point service first try to sort it out with your branch. If that doesn't work, write to the bank's head office. If you're still not satisfied the Banking Ombudsman may be able to look into the problem for you.

Cash cards may seem like licences to spend, but remember, you mustn't draw out more money than you know you have in your account unless you have arranged an overdraft.

See also: BANKS (Banking Ombudsman)

Catalogues

Mail-order catalogues are enjoying a revival. Nearly a third of all British households have at least one of them, while one in 10 has two or more. So, it's not surprising that the mail-order companies do billions of pounds worth of business every year. Today's catalogues are a far cry from the dowdy, down market digests of yesteryear. Now they are image conscious mini department stores filled with high fashion and top designs.

The main catalogue companies now have a telephone ordering service whereby the customer calls a local number to be told whether or not the item wanted is available. A predicted next stage is teleshopping where all the goods and prices will be shown on a television screen in your own home and orders placed through a small computer terminal.

Catalogues are convenient but not always cheap, though if you shop around the books you may find one or two bargains at lower-than-shop prices.

Around 90 per cent of catalogue sales through agents are on credit, and in general that is interest-free — apart from very expensive items with long repayment periods. But the interest charges are built into the advertised prices which is a reason they may seem higher than in the shops.

You might make a few friends but you won't make a fortune as an agent for a catalogue firm. If you sell only to yourself and your family the commission you receive is not subject to tax. But if you sell to friends and neighbours you could be liable to tax. Direct sales, buying straight from the company rather than through an agent, is a fast expanding side of the business.

Buying from a catalogue gives you the same rights as buying from a shop. Under the Sale of Goods Act the goods must be as described, fit for their purpose and of merchantable quality. Of course, as you haven't seen what you're buying you may not like it when it arrives. Normally if you buy at a shop you have no right to return something and get your money back just because you've changed your mind, but in practice most mail-order firms will take things back without asking why and usually say this in their advertisements, so long as you do it within a reasonable time, usually 14 days.

You are well protected if you buy from one of the major catalogue companies, who are all members of the Mail Order Traders' Association, (MOTA), 25 Castle Street, Liverpool L2 4TD, 051-236 7581. They have a code of practice which safeguards our rights. It requires that members comply with advertising codes, state prices clearly and say whether post-age and delivery are included, give 'full and clear information' about goods offered, including size, colour and materials the item is made of. It also protects us if goods are damaged in transit and allows for customers to examine goods on approval for 14 days, during which time they can return them and get a refund if they are not satisfied in any way. If the goods are not delivered on time you can cancel the order and get your money back.

If you have a complaint against a catalogue company then write to the company concerned. The address and who to complain to should be listed in the catalogue itself. If that fails, and the company is a member of MOTA, ask them to intervene. If this fails, then the case can go to arbitration under the code of practice. Your only other alternative would be to go to court, but remember you lose this option if you agree to arbitration.

If you order goods from a company that is not a member of MOTA, check the above details closely and make sure you know the address of the firm and who to complain to if something goes wrong *before* parting with your money.

See also: ADVERTISING, ARBITRATION, CODES OF PRACTICE, MAIL ORDER, SALE OF GOODS ACT

Changing Goods

A shop isn't legally obliged to exchange goods for you just because you've changed your mind. For example, if you buy a blouse only to find, when you get it home, that it doesn't match your skirt there's little you can do about it except rely on the good will of the shopkeeper.

Of course, some department stores, most notably Marks & Spencer, have a money back policy on most goods. But in law you can only insist on a refund if the goods turn out to be faulty: even then you are not entitled to an exchange. If you think you might want to swap something – maybe you're buying a present for someone and you're not sure they'll like it or you are trying to match furnishings – then check the store's policy on exchanges before you buy. If at that time they agree to change something then they are obliged to do so if you return them.

See also: SALE OF GOODS ACT

Charge Cards

A plastic card used for paying for goods and services. American Express and Diner's Club are the two best known. You pay a fee to join plus an annual charge to use them. They generally have no spending limit and you must settle what you owe, in full, each month. There are now de-luxe charge cards, called gold cards. These are usually only available to high earning bank customers and bring with them extra perks such as guaranteed overdraft facilities at lower than average rates of interest.

Cheque Cards

Also known as banker's cards and cheque guarantee cards because they do just that, they guarantee that your bank will honour a cheque up to £50 or £100. Once you've given your plastic card to the shopkeeper and he has written your card number on the back of the cheque you can't stop the cheque. As long as you have filled in the cheque correctly the bank will pay out even if you don't actually have the funds in your account – though they might not be too happy about it – and it is in fact a criminal offence to deliberately and dishonestly misuse a cheque card to get unauthorised credit. Always keep your card separately from your cheque book and if it is stolen make sure you tell your bank immediately.

See also: BANKS, CHEQUES

Cheques

If you pay by cheque you make a legally enforceable promise to pay that sum to that person. Cheques are a very convenient way of paying for things without having to carry round lots of cash, though you can't insist on someone accepting a cheque instead of cash. It's surprising how little people actually know about them, including how to fill them in correctly. First of all you should always write in ink so that it can't be rubbed out. Avoid using felt tip pen; apparently it makes it easier to trace the outline of your name for copying! Make it difficult for anyone to fraudulently tamper with the cheque by writing the words, saying how much it's for, close together. For example 'seven' cannot then be changed to 'seventy'. Draw a line through all empty spaces at the end of lines. You won't be held liable for a fraudulent cheque if you've filled it in with the usual care.

BOUNCING CHEQUES: If you haven't enough money in your account to cover the cheque the bank can refuse to pay – unless it's backed by a cheque guarantee card, in which case they have to pay up but will probably write you a nasty letter! Most banks don't worry about small amounts but don't depend on it; bouncing cheques can be embarrassing. If a bank wrongly bounces your cheque you can sue for damage to your reputation, if you can prove such damage or you're in business when it is presumed.

POST DATING CHEQUES: Useful if someone wants a cheque from you and you want to show good faith, but don't have enough money in your account at that time. Banks aren't actually too happy about post-dated cheques but the practice is perfectly legal, and if a bank pays out before the named date, and you go into the red, then don't let them try to make you pay bank charges or interest.

STOPPING CHEQUES: Once you've promised to pay you can only really stop a cheque if what you get in return has no value. But that doesn't prevent us using this device from time to time if we suddenly change our mind. In theory if you stop a cheque the recipient can sue you for the money. If you want to stop one, ring your bank and follow it up in writing. You can't stop a cheque backed by a cheque guarantee card. Banks charge for stopping cheques.

Don't keep your cheque book and guarantee card in the same place, it makes a thief's job very easy and your bank will be very displeased. If you're asked for a blank cheque, for example if you send off for theatre tickets and don't know the price, write 'not exceeding X pounds' and 'not negotiable' on the cheque. Set the amount at what you're prepared to pay. It is, of course, safer to avoid writing blank cheques if you can.

See also: BANKS, CHEQUE CARDS

Chemists

All practising pharmacists must be registered with the Pharmaceutical Society of Great Britain (or Northern Ireland). They must have a degree in pharmacy and complete practical training under a qualified pharmacist's supervision. Highly trained, their role is not just one of counting out pills and dispensing medicines, but to offer advice, help and counselling to supplement the family doctor in our society. As well as being able to suggest off-prescription remedies for minor ailments they carry out pregnancy testing and will even make home visits to supply aids for the disabled. Their health education and advisory role is one of increasing importance as they play their part in reducing the numbers of patients in the doctor's waiting room.

The pharmacist dispenses three types of medicines. The first are available on a doctor's prescription only. The pharmacist's job is to make sure the details of the prescription are correct and are printed on computerised labels giving the name of the patient and directions for dosage. The second are pharmacy only medicines. These are available off prescription but can only be bought when the pharmacist is present. The pharmacist doesn't actually have to make the sale but has to be aware of it. Finally, there are general sale list medicines which include mild painkillers. You can even buy some of these in supermarkets, but in the case of painkillers such as aspirin they can only be sold in packets containing small quantities.

In most areas pharmacists operate a rota for out of hours opening. The nearest duty chemist's name and address should be displayed on the door of your local shop or be printed in the local newspaper.

If you want to complain about the incompetence or professional misconduct of a pharmacist write to the Secretary and Registrar of the Pharmaceutical Society of Great Britain at 1 Lambeth High Street, London SE1 7JN, 01-735 9141, at 36 York Place, Edinburgh EH1 3HU for Scotland or to the Pharmaceutical Society of Northern Ireland, 73 University Street, Belfast BT7 1HL. As well as trying to settle disputes the Society can prosecute a pharmacist in certain cases, for example, if the wrong medicine was supplied.

If you want to complain about medicines supplied to you under the National Health Service or if you think the pharmacist may be in breach of his contract of service, for example if he closes early in the evening, you can complain to your local Family Practitioner Committee (address under F in phone book), the Secretary of the local Health Board in Scotland or the chief administrative officer of the local health and social services in Northern Ireland. In each case the appropriate body can discipline the pharmacist if necessary, but can't award you compensation – for this you would have to go to court.

See also: PRESCRIPTIONS

Childminding

With more and more mums going out to work, childminding has become an essential part of many families' routine. But finding safe hands in which to leave your children can be a worrying task. There are currently 58,000 minders registered with local authorities, whose role it is to check on the suitability of a would-be minder including medical checks, character references, environmental health and fire checks and regular visits from social workers. Not all registered minders are good but the majority are and fewer illegal minders now operate.

If you are looking for a childminder the best place to start is to ask family, friends or colleagues to recommend one. If that's not possible, then the local social services department (social work department in Scotland) and, in some cases, the National Childminding Association have lists of registered people in your neighbourhood. Then all you can do is work through them. Here are a few pointers to help you:

· Always visit the minder at home.
· Is the accommodation suitable? Is there plenty of floor space plus toys

and books for different age groups? Is it clean without being unnaturally tidy? (Minders are not supposed to spend the day doing housework!)

· How old are the other children she takes and will yours fit in?
· How often does she take the children out?
· How happy and settled are the other children?
· Does she belong to a local childminding group and meet minders and mothers regularly?
· Does the charge include food? What does she feed them and when?
· Can she offer the hours you want? Many minders prefer to take part-timers – this pays better – or children of teachers who need term-time care only.
· Does she share your attitudes towards behaviour, discipline, potty training and so on?
· If you have strong views on smoking or pets, make sure you discuss these points.
· Do you like her? If not, don't employ her.

If you are thinking of becoming a childminder you may find it useful to consider the following points:
· Do you find it easy to create a routine? If not, you may find it difficult to cope with different children's demands.
· Do you have plenty of stamina? Childminders agree theirs is an exhausting job. You are always on duty, and in the evenings you have to catch up with chores you can't do during the day.
· You must be registered with your social services department, and as it can take months for them to carry out all the necessary checks, start early.
· How many children can you take? The normal rule is no more than three or four under fives, including your own, and not more than one baby. If you take part-timers' children, then you can obviously look after more children during the week. There is no rule about how many over fives you care for and many minders look after school children until their parents get home.
· Be clear about what you can offer. What age child or children would best fit into your family? What hours are you prepared to do? Are you prepared to do occasional overtime?
· Charges – local authorities and National Childminding Association Groups set guidelines, but it is entirely up to the minder and parent. A

survey in 1987 showed they ranged from 60p to £1.50 an hour with the average around 96p. Parent and minder should both sign a contract covering pay, holiday pay, sickness arrangements, permission for outings, period of notice on either side.

Helpful organisations include the National Childminding Association, 8 Masons Hill, Bromley, Kent BR2 9EY, who have useful publications and general information for both minders and parents.
Working Mothers' Association, 23 Webbs Road, London SW11 6RU – a self-help and support organisation with local groups.
The National Childcare Campaign, Wesley House, 4 Wild Court, London WC2B 5AU campaigns for better, subsidised childcare facilities, particularly nurseries.
The Workplace Nurseries Campaign, Room 205, Southbank House, Black Prince Road, London SE1 7SJ wants more workplace nurseries and offers guidance to employers on setting one up.

Children

A child's birth must be registered with the local registrar of births within 42 days. There are two types of birth certificate, one shows only the names of the child, its sex and date and place of birth and is free. For a small charge there is a full version which gives the parents' names, addresses and occupations and the mother's maiden name. Only the mother or father, or someone present at the birth like the doctor, can register the birth, but anyone can get a copy of the certificate once it has been registered. Birth certificates are available from the Chief Registrar, St Catherine's House, Strand, London WC2.

A child is usually registered in its father's name unless it is illegitimate, in which case to register it with the father's surname both the father and mother have to be present or the mother has to have an affiliation order naming the father.

Until the age of 18 a child's right to do what he or she likes is limited. Even after 18 there are some things, for example standing for Parliament or, if male, consenting to a homosexual act, that you can't do until you are 21. A full list of what, in law, you can do when, is available from the Children's Legal Centre, 20 Compton Terrace, London N1 2UN, in a leaflet called 'At What Age Can I?' price 60p. The Children's Legal Centre gives advice on how the law relates to children in general and has a series of useful publications available on various aspects of children's lives.

*

Other useful addresses are:

Child Poverty Action Group, 4th floor, 1–5 Bath Street, London
EC1V 9PY: A source of general information and advice on benefits and
social security.

The National Society for the Prevention of Cruelty to Children, 67
Saffron Hill, London EC1N 8RS, 01-242 1626.

  See also: EDUCATION, ILLEGITIMACY

Citizens Advice Bureaux

The Citizens Advice Bureaux (CAB) have offices around the country. They
can give advice on a whole range of consumer problems including how
to go about solving a dispute. Their services are free and confidential.
Although most of the staff are volunteers they have been trained and
many bureaux now have in-house solicitors or local solicitors who come
in at certain times to give free legal advice.

  Set up in 1939, as well as giving advice, the Bureau may act on your
behalf by writing a letter for you, helping you perhaps to negotiate with
a trader or trade association. They can even help and advise if you are
wanting to take a case to court but they can't actually represent you in
court. Just how far a CAB will be prepared to go may well depend on
how busy they are at that particular time. Our experience is that they are
good for basic advice but don't expect them to have the time or

manpower to conduct your complaint for you. There are more than 900 CABs. To find the nearest look under Citizens Advice Bureau in the phone book.

Clothing

If you buy something to wear which turns out to be faulty, the seam comes undone, a button is missing or a size 12 turns out to be a size 16 then you are entitled to your money back from the shop where you bought it under the Sale of Goods Act. If, on the other hand, you just decide you no longer like it then you're not entitled to anything, although some shops will give you a refund, a replacement or a credit note as a matter of good will.

Any labels in clothing should be true, whether they are instructions on how to clean the garment or a breakdown of what it is made of. A designer label has to be accurate and so on; if not the seller could be prosecuted for falsely describing the goods.

When it comes to cleaning clothes check the symbols on the label before throwing it into the washing machine. If you don't stick to the instructions you won't be able to claim your money back if it then shrinks (unless they are unclear or ambiguous). On the next page are the new washing symbols as issued by the Home Laundering Consultative Council (HLCC), 24 Buckingham Gate, London SW1E 6LB, 01-828 0744. They will also answer queries on home laundering.

See also: DRY CLEANING, SALE OF GOODS ACT, SHOES

Coaches

See: BUSES AND COACHES

Coal

Our coal mines may be owned by British Coal, but the sale of coal is in the hands of private merchants. Controlled by the Weights and Measures Act 1985, solid fuel prepacked should be sold in closed bags with the net weight clearly marked. As solid fuel contains moisture the net weight of each sack will vary according to how damp it is. If you find a sackful is particularly damp ask the merchant for an allowance for this. If you buy your fuel in unsealed bags from a vehicle then the contents of each bag should be clearly marked together with the name and address of the seller.

If you have a complaint against a coal merchant which you cannot

OLD	NEW	Examples of Application

  White cotton and linen articles without special finishes

  Cotton, linen or viscose articles without special finishes where colours are fast at 60°C

  (Not used in UK) White nylon and white polyester/cotton mixtures are included in

  Nylon; polyester/cotton mixtures; polyester cotton and viscose articles with special finishes; cotton/acrylic mixtures

  Cotton, linen or viscose articles, where colours are fast at 40°C but not at 60°C

  Acrylics, acetate and triacetate, including mixtures with wool; polyester/wool blends

  Wool, wool mixed with other fibres; silk

  (Not used in UK) See items included in and

  (Not applicable in UK)

  Handwash (Do not machine wash)

  Do not wash

settle with him, you can complain to the regional secretary of the Approved Coal Merchants Scheme whose regional offices cover the whole country. They set standards of service for the industry and require merchants who register with the scheme to keep to them. If a merchant is a member of the Approved Coal Merchants Scheme he will display one of the above signs on his lorries and premises. Look for these to be sure of a fairer deal.

If you're still not satisfied, the Domestic Coal Consumers' Council, Dean Bradley House, 52 Horseferry Road, London SW1P 2AG may be able to help. They have a special address to help deal with consumer problems, FREEPOST, London EC1B 1DT, 01-212 8953.

The Solid Fuel Advisory Service will give advice on suitable fuels, appliances and systems and has a list of SFAS registered contractors who will install solid fuel heating systems. For your nearest, look in Yellow Pages or dial 100 and ask for Freefone Real Fires.

Codes of Practice

Codes of practice are rules for their members to follow drawn up by trade associations and similar organisations, sometimes with the help of the Office of Fair Trading. They are purely voluntary and have no legal status but it may help you in a claim against a trader if you can say that he is in breach of his code. There are codes of practice for many industries including electricity, motor, furniture, mail order, photographic, travel, postal services and advertising.

The codes' aim is to improve standards of service and so provide us with a better deal. They are in addition to our legal rights. Many of the codes not only set out standards for members but also lay down methods for dealing with complaints including conciliation and low-cost arbitration schemes to settle disputes between the customer and their member. Of course, remember that in every case the trader has to be a member of the particular trade association for the code of practice to apply, which could be a good reason for dealing with him in the first place. The Office of Fair Trading publishes free leaflets outlining the various codes plus a general one on arbitration under a code of practice. These are available at local Citizens Advice Bureaux and consumer advice centres.

See also: ARBITRATION, TRADE ASSOCIATIONS

Common Law

A lot of today's consumer law is based on common or case law, law developed over the years by court decisions in actual cases. The law of contract, which forms the basis of our rights when we buy from shops, is an example of this, but over the years it has been added to by statute. Common law is a useful way for courts to adapt the law as a whole to meet changing needs of society without always having to wait for Parliament to go through the lengthy process of introducing new legislation.

Common Law Wife

. . . or husband. Society may no longer frown on couples living together without being married but the law has still not quite come to terms with it. The main differences in the legal position of a married and unmarried couple relate to the duty to maintain a partner and children, rights over children of the partnership, tax (although this will change from 1990), inheritance and wills, and eligibility for state benefit.

Community Charge

See: POLL TAX

Community Health Council

Your local Community Health Council is a useful source of information about the Health Service. They have, for example, lists of local facilities including hospitals, doctors, dentists and so on. It represents the consumer in the NHS and can assist you in complaints against hospitals or the local health authority. Look up their number under C in the phone book. In Scotland the equivalent is the Local Health Council (under H or L) while in Northern Ireland it's the District Committee.

Companies

A business can trade under any name it likes, but if it is a company, either a limited liability company with Ltd after its name or a public limited company with Plc after its name, under the Companies Act it must be registered. Don't confuse firms (partnerships) with companies, even though the firm may be called Bloggs and Co. If you want to sue a trader you need to know what type of company it is so that you know who to name in the action. For example, if it is a limited company you must take action against the registered name of the company, Bloggs Ltd or Bloggs Plc and not the directors. A company must put its registered name and address on any letters and invoices but if you're having trouble finding out who and where they are you can go in person to the Companies Registration Office, London Research Room, Companies House, 55–71 City Road, London EC1Y 1BB, 01-253 9393. There is a small charge. You can do it by post, also for a fee, by writing to the Companies Registration Office, Crown Way, Maindy, Cardiff CF4 3UZ, (0222) 388588.

See also: BANKRUPTCY

Compensation

Compensation is a payment made to make up for a loss you have suffered. Lawyers call it damages. It can apply in all sorts of circumstances from loss of health through a medical accident to loss of enjoyment of a package holiday when you arrive in your hotspot to find they're still putting the roof on your bedroom. Sometimes a firm will offer you compensation without your having to go to court, but quite often you have to fight for it through the civil courts. Your entitlement will depend on what is reasonable in the circumstances bearing in mind the size of your loss. Before taking legal action for compensation it is advisable to seek the advice of a solicitor.

See also: CRIMINAL INJURIES COMPENSATION BOARD, INJURY, SALE OF GOODS ACT

Competitions

Competitions are regulated by the Lotteries and Amusements Act and to be legal the entrant must have to exercise some skill or judgement however small. The Advertising Standards Authority has issued the British Code of Sales Promotion Practice which gives strict rules for competitions, but it is voluntary and companies do not have to comply with it. The code says, among other things, that the competition must give conditions of entry including a closing date, information on the number of prizes offered and what they are, guidance on any restrictions on age or geographical area eligibility and the criteria for judging the entries as well as whether a cash alternative to any prize is available and how the results will be announced and winners notified.

If you have a complaint about a competition which cannot be sorted out with the company involved and which you think might be in breach of the code, contact the ASA, Brook House, 2–16 Torrington Place, London WC1E 7HN, 01-580 5555.

See also: JUNK MAIL, LOTTERIES

Complaining

When it comes to complaining we British could take a leaf out of our European friends' books. Can you imagine a Frenchman quietly eating a poor meal in a restaurant or a German putting up with faulty workmanship on his car? Not likely. But so often we would rather moan about the inconvenience than suffer the embarrassment of complaining.

To complain successfully first you need to know your rights. These are set out in the Sale of Goods Act 1979 and the Supply of Goods and Services Act 1982 (see SERVICES). Then you need to know who to complain to. If the problem is about something you've bought then complain to the shop, not the manufacturer. If it's a service complain to the firm that carried out the work. Speak to the boss in each case and, if necessary, put your claim in writing, keeping a copy of all letters.

Be firm, stand your ground and don't be put off by disinterest or even downright rudeness. If the shop or firm is not helpful and they have a head office, write to them outlining your complaint.

Page 56 shows a sample letter to follow when complaining.

If you still don't get a satisfactory answer complain to your local trading standards office or consumer advice centre. It could be that the trader has broken the law in some way or that there have been other complaints about him. Your final resort would be to take your complaint to court, but before doing this take legal advice. Your local Citizens Advice Bureau (under C in the phone book) would be able to advise you.

See also: SALE OF GOODS ACT, SERVICES, SMALL CLAIMS

Consumer Advice Centres

These centres were set up by the Local Government Act 1972 as part of the local authority trading standards service. By the early 1980s there were more than 100 CACs but this has now shrunk to around 50 in the wake of cutbacks in local authority spending. They work closely with Citizens Advice Bureaux and specialise in complaints about goods and services. They will sometimes take up a case for you with the shop or

If you write to a shop about faulty goods it's important to put in all the details, such as the date of purchase and the price. Using offensive language or making derogatory comments won't help your cause. Be as businesslike as possible in your approach. Here's a sample letter . . .

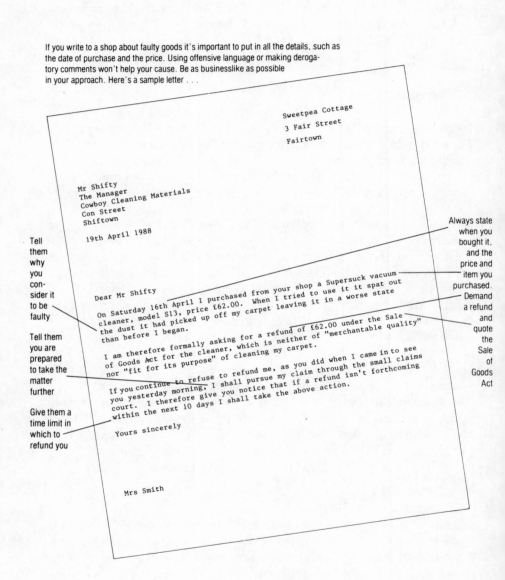

Sweetpea Cottage
3 Fair Street
Fairtown

Mr Shifty
The Manager
Cowboy Cleaning Materials
Con Street
Shiftown

19th April 1988

Dear Mr Shifty

On Saturday 16th April I purchased from your shop a Supersuck vacuum cleaner, model S13, price £62.00. When I tried to use it it spat out the dust it had picked up off my carpet leaving it in a worse state than before I began.

I am therefore formally asking for a refund of £62.00 under the Sale of Goods Act for the cleaner, which is neither of "merchantable quality" nor "fit for its purpose" of cleaning my carpet.

If you continue to refuse to refund me, as you did when I came in to see you yesterday morning, I shall pursue my claim through the small claims court. I therefore give you notice that if a refund isn't forthcoming within the next 10 days I shall take the above action.

Yours sincerely

Mrs Smith

Tell them why you consider it to be faulty

Tell them you are prepared to take the matter further

Give them a time limit in which to refund you

Always state when you bought it, and the price and item you purchased.

Demand a refund and quote the Sale of Goods Act

trader and, in theory, will accompany you to court if necessary, but in practice staff shortages might mean this is not always possible. CACs are mostly found in major cities. Check with your local council to see if there is one in your area.

Consumer Credit Act

The Consumer Credit Act 1974 tries to ensure that we get a fair deal when we obtain credit facilities – loans, hire purchase, credit cards and so on – or hire goods. It controls who can offer credit, advertising, how credit agreements are drawn up, how they are ended and what a lender can do if we default on payments.

One very important right the Act gives us is that it may allow us to claim against the lender of the money, as well as the trader who supplied the goods or services, if something goes wrong. This is in addition to our contractual rights for example, under the Sale of Goods Act.

So, if you buy a video with a personal loan from a finance company or pay by credit card such as Access, Barclaycard or Trustcard, and it is faulty, first go back to the trader. If he refuses or fails to help you, for example if he has gone bust, then make your claim against the finance company or bank. To be able to claim under Section 75 of the CCA what you bought has to have a cash price of more than £100 but less than £30,000. The loan or credit limit must be for no more than £15,000 (though the total cost of the goods or services might be). If you paid by credit card then the card has to have been taken out or renewed after 1 July 1977, when Section 75 came into force. If your card was first taken out before that date you may get less protection – that is what the credit card company may argue – and if they aren't honouring the agreement consider getting rid of your old card and taking out a new agreement. You need only have paid the deposit by credit card to claim against the finance company but there must be a connection between the trader and the lender. For example, the trader must have arranged the loan or accepted the credit card. You couldn't claim against the credit company if you'd drawn cash on your card to pay for the goods, nor against your bank if you bought the goods with a bank personal loan arranged by yourself. Section 75 doesn't apply either to charge cards where the account is settled in full each month.

Remember, it's best to try to settle the dispute with the trader first and only enlist the help of the credit company if that fails.

See also: COOLING-OFF PERIODS, CREDIT, INTEREST RATES

Consumer Groups
See: NATIONAL FEDERATION

Consumer Protection
See: TRADING STANDARDS

Consumers' Association
Publishers of the well-known *Which?* magazine, the Consumers' Association lobbies industry and government for changes in consumer protection and gives help and advice on consumer and legal matters to members. For an annual subscription fee you can join Which? Personal Service whose team will help you through consumer and legal problems, including advice on drafting letters and even helping you to take a case to court. They will also use their influence, which is quite considerable, to intervene on your behalf with retailers, manufacturers or suppliers and, if they consider your case has wider significance for consumers, may even consider paying your legal costs to see the case through.

Which? magazine is published monthly and is available on subscription. It is a very useful compendium of what to buy, from washing machines to life insurance. It has special supplements including *Holiday Which?*, *Money Which?*, *Gardening Which?*, *Motoring Which?* and, at the end of each financial year, a *Tax-Saving Which?*

If you want more information about joining the Consumers' Association write to them at 2 Marylebone Road, London NW1 4DX, 01-486 5544.

Cookers
As with any other household appliance, if you buy a cooker and find out that there is something wrong with it, that it is not as described, of merchantable quality or fit for its purpose, then you can claim your money back from the shop where you bought it under the Sale of Goods Act. If it is something simple that is wrong you may be willing to accept a repair, but this could affect your Sale of Goods rights so always make it clear to the shop that you'll insist on having your money back if the repair doesn't put the cooker right.

When buying a new cooker look for either the BSI or BEAB signs of approval. All gas cookers with British Standards Institution certification and all electric cookers passed by the British Electrotechnical Approvals

Board have undergone stringent safety checks. All cookers sold by British Gas and by Electricity Boards are approved in this way.

See also: ELECTRICITY, GAS

Cooling-off Periods

Usually once you've signed a contract for something you can't just change your mind and back out. However, thanks to the Consumer Credit Act, if you sign a credit agreement somewhere other than at a trader's business premises, for example, at your home, you have a certain time in which you can change your mind. This is called a 'cooling-off period'. The idea of the 'cooling-off period' is to protect us from over-zealous door-to-door salesmen who might bamboozle us into parting with money for something we don't really want.

When you first sign the credit agreement you should be given a copy of it. Then, usually within a week, you'll be sent, by post, a notice outlining your cancellation rights. Once this arrives you have five days, starting the day after you receive the notice, in which to write to the lender to cancel the agreement if you wish to do so. If you do cancel it's a good idea to send the letter by recorded delivery or some other postal method which gives you proof of posting in case the letter doesn't arrive.

If you cancel you must then return any goods you have already received because of the agreement. You'll be entitled to get back any deposit you have paid.

Some lenders will allow you a 'cooling-off period' even when you're not entitled in law, for example if you sign the agreement at a trader's premises. So if you're in doubt it's always worth checking what the arrangements are should you change your mind, before you sign.

Cosmetics

By law cosmetics must be safe. They should not contain harmful substances and in normal use should not be a danger to our health. Their manufacture, sale and labelling is governed by legislation. The Cosmetic Products (Safety) Regulations 1984 (amended 1985) list more than 350 ingredients, including lead, which may no longer be used in making cosmetics and limits the use of many others to small amounts. A manufacturer in breach of these regulations can be prosecuted.

Council Homes

For general advice on housing ask at your local Citizens Advice Bureau (under C in the phone book). They have useful leaflets on housing matters and can point you in the right direction if you need further help. Some local authorities have housing aid and advice centres specifically to answer enquiries about housing. Ask your local council if there is one in your area.

Shelter is a national pressure group which advises on virtually any housing matter and it will sometimes take up a complaint on your behalf. Contact Shelter, the National Campaign for the Homeless at 157 Waterloo Road, London SE1 8XF, 01-633 9377 for details of regional offices. Shelter may be able to help you with a complaint about council housing which hasn't been resolved with the local authority department itself.

The most common problems concerning council housing are failing to house someone and failing to maintain property. A local authority has a duty to help people who are homeless or who fear they will be shortly. But unless you are an urgent case their help may only amount to advice. If you think you haven't received the help you're entitled to, then complain to your local authority's Director of Housing. If that doesn't sort it out then you could ask your local councillor to look into the matter for you or ask the Local Ombudsman to investigate.

The Council has an obligation to carry out necessary maintenance and repair work to their property. If you need work done write to the housing department telling them what is wanted and give them a reasonable time to do it in. If it isn't done you could get your own estimates and send the cheapest to the housing department again telling them they should do the work within a specified time, say a couple of weeks, or you will have the work done yourself and deduct the cost from your rent.

If a matter of health is involved, for example you have extensive damp, you could call in the environmental health department and ask their inspector to try to put pressure on the housing department on your behalf. If the work is major you could go as far as taking the council to court, or at least threatening to do so, for breaking their legal obligations to maintain the property. If you need to do this get legal advice first.

See also: HOUSING, LOCAL AUTHORITIES, OMBUDSMEN

Councils
See: LOCAL AUTHORITIES

Counterfeiting
Contraceptive pills that don't work, bogus brake linings that could cause a fatal crash – the world-wide market in fake goods has, in recent years, gone far beyond cheap tapes and designer look-alike teeshirts. While counterfeiters concentrated on copies of designer label jeans sold in street markets and poor man's Chanel perfume, the consumer wasn't necessarily getting a poor deal. After all the buyer might be getting a low quality reproduction but it was cheap – only the original manufacturer could be missing out by losing trade. But suddenly wider safety issues are involved. For example, as well as fake birth control pills a report from the European Parliament recounted how bogus components were found in 600 helicopters supplied to NATO countries including Britain. Closer to our homes are dangerous children's toys – cheap imports made to look like their more expensive authentic counterparts but not made to the same high safety standards.

The fake business is now worth about £60 billion or six per cent of all world trade. In the front line in this country, fighting the fakers, are trading standards and consumer protection officers. If you think you've spotted counterfeits on sale report it to them at the local town hall or council offices. Working against the fakers on behalf of the industry is an anti-counterfeiting group, whose members are firms which have had trouble with copycats. They want to see the law tightened to plug the loopholes clever fakers currently exploit, while on an international scale the Counterfeiting Intelligence Bureau is tracking down fakers all around the world in an effort to stop these goods reaching the market.

To avoid buying fakes:
· Be suspicious of goods bought from market stalls at very low prices. Watch out for incorrect spelling in brand names.
· In clothing watch out for skimpy cutting and wrong size labels.
· Video tapes. This is a big market. Look out for printing on labels which isn't clear, also photocopied labels.

Courts
Settling a dispute in court is a time-consuming business but sometimes it is the only avenue left to pursue our rights. A word of warning though –

only go to court if everything else has failed to sort out your problem and, unless you have a good grasp of the law and court procedures, take legal advice first. Half an hour of a solicitor's time needn't cost the earth if you use the Fixed Fee Interview Scheme.

Whether you go it alone or seek legal help you should consider the following points:
· Have you a good case and are you likely to win? A solicitor could be a big help here as he knows the points that could help decide the case in your favour.
· Is the person worth suing? Does he or she have money to pay you if you win?
· Can you afford it? Although usually the loser pays costs, even if you win you may have to meet your own costs initially.
· Once you've started the action are you prepared to go through with it? It isn't easy to duck out once the court machine has rolled into motion.

Most consumer complaints are civil cases and are heard in the County Court so long as they are for claims under £5,000. (Claims over that would be heard in the Crown Court.) Claims for less than £500 are heard under the special Small Claims procedure of the County Court. In Scotland civil claims are heard in the Sheriff's Court and while there is no equivalent of small claims there is a simplified system for claims under £1,000 called summary cause. In Northern Ireland civil claims under £2,000 are heard in the County Court while there are, once again, less formal hearings for claims under £300. Claims must be brought to court within a specified time after they have arisen so don't delay too long. Also, make sure you have tried to settle out of court and have given the trader written notice of your intention to sue – that quite often does the trick without actually going to court. You can get details of how to take a case to court from your local County Court office or Citizens Advice Bureau (both under C in the phone book).

   Criminal prosecutions, for example if a local authority trading standards department prosecutes a trader, are heard in the Magistrates' Court (Sheriff's Court in Scotland) or the Crown Court (High Court in Scotland). In both civil and criminal cases the court may award compensation to a wronged consumer.

   See also: COMPENSATION, FIXED FEE INTERVIEW, SMALL CLAIMS

Credit

A third of consumer spending in Britain, not counting mortgages, is done on credit. And even if you don't flash a wallet full of credit cards the chances are that at some time your bank account has slipped into the red. But the easy terms can come a bit too easy for some. And the irony is that the more credit you have already the more you are likely to be offered. The spread of the high street credit habit is one of the reasons why some people take on more borrowing than they can really afford.

Nearly every shop in the high street nowadays wants to lend us money. It seems that no self-respecting chain store is without a plastic card of its own. Used carefully these cards can be a real help with household budgeting, spreading the cost of expensive items and helping us buy things for which we would otherwise have had to save for months.

Here are some dos and don'ts of credit to prevent you slipping over the red line into debt.

BEFORE YOU TAKE ON A LOAN DO . . .

· work out what it will cost you. You may find you are paying double the cash price.
· check the APR (annual percentage rate). This figure is a measure of the price of the credit and includes the interest you'll pay plus hidden charges such as arrangement fees. By law the APR has to be given. It enables you to compare the cost of credit and some credit cards have nearly twice the APR of others.
· make sure that you can afford the repayments. Work out your current income and outgoings before taking on a new commitment.
· remember you have the right to cancel a credit agreement signed in your own home up to five days after receiving a copy of the agreement through the post.

IF YOU GET INTO PROBLEMS OWING MONEY DON'T . . .

· get priorities wrong. It's important to pay rates, mortgage or rent and heating bills before credit payments. The fact that the credit company might be chasing you hardest doesn't mean that debt must be paid first.
· leave it too late to get help. Start with a visit to your local Citizens Advice Bureau. Many now have specially trained debt counsellors and even if they don't, they will still be able to point you in the right direction for help.
· take on a new loan to pay the old one. It could make things a lot worse. Some finance companies specialise in lending money to pay debts, at exorbitant interest rates.
· ever give up your child benefit book to someone who offers to help.
· write long sob stories to the credit company. But do write and tell them *briefly* of your difficulties. Explain the circumstances and tell them what you intend to do about it, for example, how much you think, realistically, you can afford to pay each week or month. Don't be afraid to offer small amounts, anything is better than nothing, all the credit company wants is to get its money back. Keep them informed – some credit companies will freeze interest payments in extreme circumstances.

Anyone who offers credit has to be licensed by the Office of Fair Trading and it is a criminal offence to trade without a licence. If you have a complaint against a lender try to sort it out with the office or branch where the loan was granted. Failing that, write to their head office. If you're getting nowhere contact your local trading standards department. It could be that the lender is in breach of the Consumer Credit Act, in which case he could be prosecuted. If you think your credit charges are extortionate you can take the matter to court, which might reduce your payments.

See also: BORROWING, CONSUMER CREDIT ACT, CREDIT CARDS, CREDIT REFERENCE

Credit Cards

Plastic credit cards, such as Access and Barclaycard, are widely used to pay for goods and services both at home and abroad. You are given a credit limit and each month are sent a statement. You must pay the minimum amount shown on the bottom of the statement, but if you pay the balance in full, before the date it is due, you don't have to pay any

*Take a card...
any card...*

interest. Interest is charged on any outstanding balance. Clever use of credit cards can give you up to eight weeks of interest-free credit. But once paying, interest on credit cards is high.

If you use your card for a cash advance you don't get this interest-free period. Some companies charge interest on the sum immediately, others charge a percentage handling fee.

If your card is lost or stolen inform the credit company immediately. As long as you inform them straight away and then confirm it in writing, you should not be liable for any misuse of the card.

It's always worth checking regularly that you have all your cards. Don't forget to doublecheck that you've been given the correct card back in restaurants and shops and keep all receipts to check against your statement when it arrives. Tell the company straight away if you find a payment on your statement that you don't think you made and ask them to check it for you.

Credit Notes

If you buy faulty goods from a shop you're entitled to your money back under the Sale of Goods Act. Don't be pushed into accepting a credit note instead. A credit note is a voucher which allows you to purchase other goods up to its value from the same shop – but you might not want to buy again from a shop that sold you something faulty in the first place. If, on the other hand, you just change your mind and want to exchange the goods for something else then the shop would be doing you a favour by offering you a credit note as, in law, it needn't give you anything.

Credit Reference

Before a trader gives you credit he may ask a credit reference agency about you. These agencies collect information about people's financial standing including bad debts. If you are turned down for credit it could be because you appear on one of these agencies' lists. Under the Consumer Credit Act you are entitled to know whether or not a trader has consulted an agency about your financial standing, and you can ask to see what is on file about you. If you are turned down, ask the trader, in writing, within 28 days of being refused, if he has consulted an agency and if so which one. He must give you its name and address within seven days. You should then write to them and demand to see a copy of any file on you. You will have to give the agency your name and any addresses over the last few years and you will have to pay a small fee. If the information is incorrect or misleading you can have it changed or removed. Any changes should then be sent to anyone who has been given the incorrect information in the past six months. You can write to a credit reference agency at any time to check if they have a file on you. For example, if you have been in dispute with a firm over a payment and fear that you have been 'blacklisted' unfairly. In some cases people have found their way on to lists just by living in a street of bad debtors or because of the bad debts of previous occupiers of the house!

Credit Unions

Credit unions are a sort of do-it-yourself bank. Members pay an amount of money into a fund each week and are allowed to borrow up to a certain limit, the amount varying according to the input, at a low rate of interest. Credit unions are savings and loans clubs formed by groups of people who share a common interest. For example, neighbours, work colleagues or sports club members. They operate on the principle that lending money is less risky to people you know and work very well when properly run. They are ideal for people who don't have bank accounts and for those who might have difficulty borrowing money through other accepted channels.

Look carefully at the credit union before you join. Some are better organised than others. There are specific rules about the number of members and the amount you can save and borrow. As a protection for your money they have to send quarterly returns to the Chief Registrar of Friendly Societies who has the authority to investigate their activities. They must also have insurance to cover fraud or dishonesty by any of their officials or employees but this doesn't cover incompetence due to inexperienced management. According to the Consumers' Association some unions have had problems because their officers underestimated the time and resources they would need to run the union.

Criminal Injuries Compensation Board

Set up in 1964 to provide compensation for victims of violent crime, the Criminal Injuries Compensation Board is financed by the Government and administered by an independent board of lawyers.

You can apply for compensation if you were injured . . .

· as a result of violent crime
· trying to stop someone committing a crime
· trying to apprehend a suspect after a crime
· trying to help the police apprehend someone

You can claim even though someone hasn't been brought to justice for the crime. You must apply within three years of the date you were injured and to prevent claims for trivial injuries the claim must be for £400 or more. You can't usually claim for traffic accidents. You can only claim for personal injuries and not for damage to property or goods. But you can claim if you are the dependant of someone who dies because of injuries received in any of these circumstances. Forms for making your claim, plus an explanatory leaflet, are available from the Criminal Injuries Compensation Board, Whittington House, 19–30 Alfred Place, Chenies Street, London WC1E 7LG.

D

Dangerous Goods

An iron that becomes live when it's plugged in, curling tongs that set your hair alight and a child's toy buggy which slices off fingertips are just a few of the innocent looking but highly dangerous goods which have been on sale in Britain recently. Although most goods are perfectly safe in themselves, with some becoming potentially dangerous when mis-used, there are thousands which are deadly. Many of the worst offenders are on sale on market stalls, often cheap imports from the Far East, where manufacturing standards are not always as high as our own.

The Consumer Protection Act 1987 imposes a duty on all suppliers of goods, both manufacturers and retailers, to ensure that goods are safe. But the retailer has a defence if he didn't know, nor had reasonable grounds for believing that the goods weren't safe. The Act is designed to cover goods not previously covered by safety standards or regulations but doesn't extend to secondhand goods. Although a wide variety of goods, from paraffin heaters to pushchairs, are covered by British Standards set by the British Standards Institution, many items are not, which until the Consumer Protection Act allowed for loopholes letting dangerous goods sneak their way into the shops. The Act also empowers customs officers to seize goods at ports if they suspect they are unsafe and trading standards officers have greater powers to check suspect goods.

So far we have dealt with what is done to prevent dangerous goods going on sale, but if you actually buy something which you think, or know, isn't safe take it back to the shop where you bought it. Also report it to your local trading standards or consumer protection department (under your local authority or Regional Council in the phone book).

Both the shopkeeper and the official can then take action, if necessary, to stop others buying them. Under the Sale of Goods Act, you are entitled to your money back from the shop where you bought the goods, as something which is dangerous is not of merchantable quality. You might also be able to claim compensation against either the shop or the manufacturer, or both. This has been made easier under the Consumer Protection Act, which says that manufacturers, and importers from non-EEC countries will be responsible for injury or damage caused by their defective products regardless of whether they are at fault or not. If you think you might be entitled to compensation then seek legal advice.

See also: BRITISH STANDARDS INSTITUTION, GOODS, PRODUCT LIABILITY

Data Protection Act
See: INFORMATION

Date Stamping
In law, manufacturers are obliged to mark food products with 'best before' dates. But there is nothing to stop shopkeepers from leaving food on the shelves after the date has expired. The date is just meant to be a guideline and most manufacturers tend to err on the side of caution. It is, however, illegal to sell food which is unwholesome or unfit for consumption and if you think a shop is guilty of this then report them to your local trading standards or consumer protection department.

Death
Amid the grief and pain when you lose someone close to you there are many practical things which have to be done and important arrangements to be made. As well as having to have the death certified, and registering it, you'll have to decide quickly whether your loved one should be buried or cremated, you'll have to deal with the undertakers and may have to sort through the red tape of pensions, state benefits and insurance policies.

Here's a guide to what to do, when to do it, and who can help you.

FIRST CALL YOUR FAMILY DOCTOR. If you can't get hold of him or her, dial 999 and ask for the ambulance service, explain why. You should do this straight away unless the person has been ill for some time and the doctor is aware of this. In such a case, if the death is at three in the morning you could wait until a reasonable hour to call. Tell the doctor if the person is to be cremated as a second doctor will be required to see the body.

REGISTER THE DEATH. Every death has to be registered with the local registrar of births and deaths in the area where it took place. A list of local registrars is usually pinned up in doctors' surgeries. To register the death you have to have a medical certificate of the cause of death, usually issued by the doctor who has been looking after the patient during the final illness. This certificate is free and states not only the probable cause of death but also the last date the person was seen alive and also certifies that the doctor actually saw the body.

In England and Wales, unless there are special circumstances, deaths should be registered within five days. Although this is usually done by a relative, anyone present at the death or who knew about the last illness or who lived in the same house as the deceased can register it. If you are related then you only need to live in the same sub-district of the registrar to do it.

When you go along to the registrar's office you'll need to take with you the cause of death certificate and, if possible, the person's birth and marriage certificates and their national health service medical card. These aren't vital but they contain a lot of information the registrar will need.

MAKE SURE YOU HAVE THE RIGHT DOCUMENTS. Once the death has been registered you will need to get a number of certificates from the registrar. A certificate showing that you have registered the death is available free and you'll need it if you want to claim national insurance benefits. The standard death certificate, price £2, is necessary for getting probate and for insurance and pension purposes. Certain other special certificates might be necessary if you need to prove death – for example to get money from the deceased's Friendly Society account.

If you have with you a list of any occasions when you might have to prove the death, the registrar will be able to advise you. You can get death certificates at a later date but it could cost you more.

SEE AN UNDERTAKER. After calling the doctor your next call will probably be to an undertaker who will then deal with the body and make arrangements for either burial or cremation. If you don't know of an undertaker you could ask your doctor or else the National Association of Funeral

Directors, 57 Doughty Street, London WC1N 2NE, 01-242 9388, for a list of their members in your area. Members observe a code of practice which helps ensure that consumers get a good deal.

Burial: When a death is registered, the registrar will issue a green certificate (the disposal certificate), which means you can go ahead and bury the person or apply for cremation. Until this point you can only make provisional plans for the funeral.

Cremation: There are extra formalities which have to be gone through if the person is to be cremated. Four forms, available from the crematorium or the funeral directors, have to be filled in – one by the next of kin or executor and the others by three different doctors. It is because of the extra need for certificates of death that you should make it known to your doctor at the outset that the person wished to be cremated.

CHECK IF YOU ARE ENTITLED TO ANY BENEFITS. You may be eligible for state benefits if your spouse or a close relative dies. Check with your local department of health and social security office (under H in the phone book) or ring the DHSS Freefone, 0800 666 555.

UNEXPECTED DEATH. So far we've looked at what to do if someone dies in normal circumstances, but things are slightly different if the death is unexpected, the result of an accident or the person dies while in hospital.

If a doctor hasn't been seeing the deceased during his or her last illness, the death will have to be reported to the coroner. Even if a doctor has been visiting, the coroner will have to be told if the deceased was not seen within the last 14 days. The coroner will then look into the matter and decide whether there should be a post mortem or an inquest.

Deaths which are sudden and unexplained, which occurred in suspicious circumstances – for example if a crime might have been committed – or as the result of an accident, together with suicides and deaths while in prison or police custody must all be reported to the coroner. You can report it yourself by telephoning the police station or ask your doctor to do it.

IN HOSPITAL. If someone dies while in hospital, the hospital's administrative staff will usually help with all the necessary formalities, and a hospital doctor will probably complete the medical certificate of cause of death.

AND IN SCOTLAND
If someone dies in Scotland the procedure is much the same except that you have to register the death within 8 days and this can be done either in the area where the person died *or* in the area where he or she normally lived. There is no coroner but his duties are carried out by a procurator fiscal. Post mortems are much rarer in Scotland where external medical examinations are most often relied upon to find out why someone died.

For more details ask at your local DHSS office for leaflet D49, *What to Do After Death*. There is a similar leaflet for Scotland. The following organisations may also be helpful:

Cruse, 126 Sheen Road, Richmond, Surrey TW9 1UR, 01-940 4818/ 9047 is an organisation which offers help and support to the bereaved. There are over 140 branches in the UK.

National Association of Widows, 1st floor, Neville House, 14 Waterloo Street, Birmingham B2 5TX, 021-643 8348 offers advice for widows.

The Compassionate Friends, Gill Hodder, 6 Denmark Street, Bristol BS1 5DQ, (0272) 292778, is an organisation that helps those whose children have died.

Debt
See: CREDIT

Decorators
As with all services, where you pay someone to carry out a job for you, a decorator should do the work with reasonable care and skill, within a reasonable time and at a reasonable price. If you want the work done within a set time this should be made clear at the beginning. Your rights are set out in the Supply of Goods and Services Act and although all the details of the Act do not apply in Scotland, you have similar rights there under common law.

When making an agreement with a decorator, get it in writing and find out if the price includes materials. If he supplies the paint then it must be as described, of merchantable quality and fit for its purpose, under the Sale of Goods Act. If it isn't you have a claim against the decorator.

Some decorators are members of the British Decorators' Association. If you have a complaint against a member the Association will look into it for you. If the complaint is about the standard of work they can inspect it for you and make a report which would be useful evidence in court if your complaint got that far. Always try to sort out your problem with the individual decorator or company first.

The British Decorators' Association is at 6 Haywra Street, Harrogate HG1 5BL, (0423) 67292/3.

Delivery Dates

Shops can be irritatingly vague about delivery dates, particularly if they have to order goods for you from manufacturers. Generally speaking unless a specific date has been agreed, goods have to be delivered within a reasonable time, but what is reasonable would depend on individual circumstances. For example, if you order a bookcase and are told it will be about 12 weeks before it is delivered then 14 weeks might be reasonable, but if you are told delivery would be in a few days, 6 weeks might be viewed as unreasonable. If you think you've waited long enough, write to the trader and give him a set time, say 10 days, in which to deliver or inform him that you consider the contract cancelled and you want your money back.

If when you order the goods you want them by a certain date – for example, if you're ordering champagne for a wedding – make this clear at the outset. Put in writing that 'time is of the essence'. The legal jargon makes it easier to argue your case if dispute should arise, and if the trader fails to meet the date you can cancel the contract and demand your money back from him. You may also have a claim for damages if an agreed date has not been met and you have suffered a loss as a result.

Dentists

Just the thought of going to the dentist is enough to set most people's teeth on edge so it's important to find one that you're happy with. If you're looking for a dentist, ask for recommendations from friends or neighbours or get a list of local dentists from your Family Practitioner Committee or Area Health Board (Scotland) or Central Services Agency (Northern Ireland). Then it's just a matter of trying them.

It's your right to get all the treatment you need to make you 'dentally fit' under the NHS. However, some dentists don't provide a full range of dental treatments on the NHS. If you don't want work done privately then make this clear from the beginning, and go to another dentist if necessary. Always get an NHS receipt for every payment.

At the time of going to press, examinations, check-ups – including advice on looking after teeth – and repairs and readjustments to dentures are free to all patients. You also get free treatment if you're under 16 (or under 19 if still in full-time education), if you're pregnant or a mother of a child under a year old or on a low income, that is in receipt of Income Support, otherwise you have to pay 75 per cent of the cost of treatment up to a maximum limit of £150.

A dentist is within his rights to refuse to treat you or to refuse to treat you on the NHS. However, if NHS treatment is refused, this must be stated before work commences.

Each time you start a course of treatment, even if it's with the same dentist, you're entering a new agreement. At the initial examination you'll be asked to sign a dental estimate form which is, in effect, a contract. This means you're giving your consent to the examination and any necessary treatment.

Find out how much the proposed treatment is likely to cost. If you don't agree, refuse further treatment. Once you've agreed, you're committed to paying the appropriate charge for all treatment carried out.

If you choose to go privately, there are no standard charges; it's up to you and your dentist to agree terms, so it's a good idea to get a written estimate before you agree to undergo treatment.

If you're not happy with your dentist – for example if you don't think the work he has recommended is really necessary – you should get a second opinion from another dentist. It's your right.

However, there is a catch. If you want treatment under the NHS, before the dentist will even examine you, you must sign the dental form which declares that you are not being treated by another dentist under the NHS and, technically, a check-up counts as treatment. So the only way to get a second opinion quickly is to end your contract with the first dentist immediately after the check-up, before the treatment begins, then start with the next. Alternatively you can ask your dentist or family doctor to refer you to another NHS dentist, but that could take months. Or there's always the option of paying for a private examination.

If you're not satisfied with dental treatment you've received, your first step should be to talk it over with your dentist and try to reach some agreement. If you're still not happy, and the treatment was under the NHS, you should report it immediately to your local Family Practitioner Committee (sister bodies as above for Scotland and N. Ireland). They can investigate dentists and discipline them if necessary and, if they think the matter is serious enough, they can report a dentist to the General Dental Council if for example the dentist was negligent.

However, these bodies can't award financial compensation (though they can order that your money should be refunded). For compensation you would have to take the matter to court. There is a lot of red tape in the complaints procedure at present, but if it's a genuine complaint it's worth pursuing, but you should seek legal advice first.

Whether your treatment has been carried out privately or on the NHS, if you believe a dentist has been guilty of serious professional misconduct, such as treating you while drunk, you can write direct to the General Dental Council, 37 Wimpole Street, London W1M 8DQ, 01-486 2171.

Deposits

Paying a deposit for goods is an act of good faith to show the shopkeeper that you intend to buy, and usually you can't recover the money if you subsequently change your mind. You can, however, get back a deposit if the trader breaks his side of the agreement – for example if he fails to get you the goods within a reasonable time.

If you have paid a deposit to a company which then goes bust there is little, in practice, you can do about it. You are entitled to your money back but will have to join a long list of unsecured creditors and will only get a refund if there is money left to pay out when most other debts have been met. If you have to pay a deposit, particularly to a firm you know little about, then ask if your money is protected by a bonding scheme which will safeguard payments if the firm does collapse or, if the total price is more than £100, pay by credit card, this way you can claim against the credit company if the trader goes out of business.

See also: ADVANCE PAYMENTS, BANKRUPTCY, CONSUMER CREDIT ACT, ESTATE AGENTS (last paragraph)

The Design Council

Set up in 1944 The Design Council is an independent, though Government-sponsored, organisation which promotes the improvement of design in products made in Britain. The Council has an advisory service which offers help and advice to British industry and encourages consumers to buy well-designed British products. The Council examines more than 4,000 products each year and those that are approved can be shown in Design Centre showrooms and carry the familiar Design Centre label. Products are judged on their performance, construction,

appearance and value for money. The Design Council, 28 Haymarket, London SW1Y 4SU, 01-839 8000 (regional offices in Glasgow, Cardiff, Belfast, Wolverhampton and Manchester) will also look into serious complaints about products carrying their label.

Discount Stores

These vary from high street showrooms to vast out-of-town ware-houses. Prices are usually lower than in ordinary shops but often you have to buy without being able to look at the goods individually. You'll probably have to pay extra if you want the goods delivered.

Discrimination

If you think you have been discriminated against because of your race or your sex you may be able to take legal action to redress the balance.

RACE: The Race Relations Act 1976 makes it unlawful to discriminate against someone because of their colour, race, nationality or ethnic origins. It isn't actually a criminal offence but anyone who thinks they've been the victim of discrimination has the right to take legal action through an industrial tribunal (for matters of employment) or through the County Court, Sheriff Court in Scotland, for any other matters. The Commission for Racial Equality, Elliot House, 10−12 Allington Street, London SW1E 5EH, 01-828 7022 will give advice and help to anyone who thinks they might have grounds for a complaint.

SEX: The Sex Discrimination Act 1975 makes it unlawful for anyone to be treated less favourably than another because of their sex. Although we usually hear the Act mentioned in relation to women it does apply equally to men. As with racial discrimination, the Act gives you the right to go to an industrial tribunal or County Court but doesn't actually make discrimination a criminal offence.

The Equal Opportunities Commission is the statutory body set up to help in cases of sex discrimination. Their head office is Overseas House, Quay Street, Manchester M3 3HN, 061-833 9244 plus regional offices at Caerwys House, Windsor Place, Cardiff CF1 1LB, and St Andrew's House, 141 West Nile Street, Glasgow GW1 2RN.

If you want to complain about an advert which you think is racist or sexist, then contact the appropriate Commission.

See also: EQUAL OPPORTUNITIES

District Committee (Northern Ireland)
See: COMMUNITY HEALTH

Divorce
Under today's divorce laws virtually everyone who wants a divorce can get one, and for the most part the idea of blame or any 'guilty party' has gone. During the 1980s the divorce statistics rose, with one in three marriages now being dissolved.

The only ground for divorce is the irretrievable breakdown of the marriage. You have to show one or more of the following to prove this: that your partner has committed adultery and you find it intolerable to live with him or her; that he or she has behaved unreasonably (which can be anything from cutting toe nails in bed to hitting you); that you have been deserted; that you have been separated for two years (when you both agree to the divorce) or you have been separated for five years (when you can divorce without your partner's consent).

If you haven't been married long and don't have complicated property settlements or any children, you can do your own divorce which is both cheap and simple. Forms and details of what to do are available from your local County Court. But even with a 'quickie' divorce you might benefit from some basic legal advice, which can be cheap if you find a solicitor who operates the Fixed Fee Interview or Green Form scheme (see appropriate sections).

If you consult a solicitor, remember that you pay by the hour, so go prepared. Take with you a list of all your assets and liabilities, including details of your house, property, financial arrangements including mortgage, bank accounts, wills, insurances, stocks and shares and any other income you have. Also have details of your earnings and, if possible, those of your spouse. The solicitor is there to help you sort out the details and *not* to act as a marriage guidance counsellor. Circumstances of divorce vary and in reaching a settlement the court will take into account, among other things, the needs of children, of yourself and your spouse, and the income of the family. If there are children the court will have to be satisfied that they have been adequately provided for before granting a decree nisi. Once the decree nisi has been granted you have to wait six weeks for the decree absolute, during which time either of you can change your mind. After the decree absolute, then you are legally divorced. Scottish divorces are final as soon as they are granted; you will receive a copy of the divorce decree.

If you are separated or divorced you are entitled to financial help from the state in respect of the children as if you were single. These could include child and one parent family benefits. Also, if you're a lone parent, ask the tax office about the Additional Personal Allowance.

See also: BENEFITS, FIXED FEE INTERVIEW, GREEN FORM SCHEME, ONE PARENT FAMILIES, TAX

Doctors

You can register as a patient with any doctor who will accept you. If for some reason you fall out and want to see another one, within a group practice you can usually ask to see one of the other doctors. If you want to change your doctor completely, you can either get your present doctor's signature on your medical card agreeing to the change or send your card to your local Family Practitioner Committee, the Central Services Agency in Northern Ireland or the area Health Board in Scotland, telling them you want to change. They will tell you what to do next. You're not allowed to consult your National Health Service GP privately but you can go to another as a private patient without coming off the list of your NHS doctor.

If you move to a new area and want to find a doctor, either ask friends if they can recommend one or request a list of doctors registered in your area from the local Family Practitioner Committee (as above for Scotland and Northern Ireland). You will usually be expected to register with a doctor serving your area and only if he or she agrees to continue treating you will you be able to stay with them if you move away.

If you have a complaint against a doctor about the standard of care given, for example that he or she wouldn't visit you at home, first give them a chance to sort it out. If this fails ask the FPC (or others as listed above) to look into it. Complaints of a more serious nature such as a doctor's behaviour including drunkenness or assault should be reported to the General Medical Council, the governing body of the profession, at 44 Hallam Street, London W1N 6AE, 01-580 7642. They can go as far as striking a doctor off the medical register. If you believe you are entitled to compensation you can sue your doctor for negligence, whether you're a private or NHS patient, but in practice this can be a lengthy and difficult process so always seek legal advice.

When you visit your doctor, or go into hospital, it can feel as if you're losing all rights over your body. But this isn't so. Here are a few of the things you can say 'no' to: you don't have to talk to your doctor in front of a student who is 'sitting in' on the surgery; in hospital you can say 'no' to students too, though in a teaching hospital it may be assumed you don't mind but if you do, don't be afraid to say so; a consultant should ask first if the students are to examine you and you can refuse. You can refuse too the suggested treatment itself, but bear in mind that if you do the consultant can discharge you even if you're still ill, unless your objections are 'reasonable'.

If you want a second opinion you can't force your GP (General Practitioner) to refer you to a specialist, though, of course, you could choose to pay to see one privately. If you're referred to a consultant you can't insist on seeing the top man himself nor that he actually does an operation, and you have no automatic right to know the results of hospital tests on you.

A doctor or midwife can ask a father to leave if the delivery of a baby is a difficult one.

All GPs must arrange 24-hour medical cover for their patients, though they needn't be available themselves; and in an emergency a GP must treat you even if you're not on his or her list.

See also: DENTISTS, HOSPITALS, INFORMATION (for Data Protection Act)

Dogs

Is your neighbour's dog keeping you awake at night barking? Has it frightened or attacked you or your children? If so the owner could be prosecuted.

Dog owners have a legal obligation to control their animals in various ways. For example, in some areas local authority bye-laws can fine someone for allowing their dog to foul the footpath. So, if you want someone to be prosecuted for this report them to the police or the local authority. The dog owner does, however, have a defence if he, or she, can show that they took reasonable steps to take the animal to the road or even to the grass verge, as some court cases have shown. If a dog runs amok in your garden and you can show that the owner did nothing to prevent this you might be able to sue him for trespass and claim compensation. In Scotland – where there is no law of trespass – you might try to bring a case, with the help of your neighbours, under the Civic Government (Scotland) Act 1980.

Local bye-laws may also apply to dogs barking or being unreasonably noisy at night. If the local authority won't prosecute you can take the owner to court yourself, but first give him or her reasonable opportunity to quieten their animal. If this doesn't work you need to serve formal notice on them, saying that they have a certain amount of time in which to put the matter right, a few weeks is probably reasonable. The notice should be signed by at least three other householders affected by the noise and sent by recorded delivery to make sure it arrives.

If your problem is a dangerous dog then the owner can be prosecuted under the Dogs Act 1871. Usually the local authority or police will deal with it if you report the matter, but failing that you can bring a private prosecution. As with all private prosecutions it is best to seek legal advice first – your local Citizens Advice Bureau will be able to advise you.

See also: NEIGHBOURS (Cats and dogs).

Doorstep Sales

Rarely are we more vulnerable to heavy sales pressure than when the salesman comes to our home. Sometimes we only end up with a cheap set of brushes or a can of furniture polish, at other times we can be persuaded to part with thousands of pounds for double glazing or a new roof.

Here are a few tips on how to deal with a doorstep salesman:
· Don't agree to anything, least of all sign a contract, without thinking about it overnight. No matter how enthusiastic you might be – particularly if the over zealous salesman is trying to lure you with discounts if you sign immediately – it is better to play safe now than be sorry later.
· Watch out for salesmen masquerading as market researchers. This is a clever way to get past your door so don't be afraid to ask them to leave

once you've found out the true purpose of their call. Genuine market researchers show identification and don't sell.

· Be suspicious. Is the person really selling something or are they just wanting to get into your house for some other dubious purpose? Tales of bogus door-to-door salesmen 'casing' the homes of elderly people for accomplices to come back and burgle are not unheard of.

· Always ask to see some form of identification before asking anyone into your home and don't be afraid to shut the door in their face if they persist.

· If you really must buy then try to do so on credit. It's usually easy to change to paying by cash later if you want, but in the meantime you can take advantage of the 'cooling-off period' credit offers. If you sign a credit agreement away from business premises, such as in the home, then, so long as you do it quickly, you can change your mind (see CONSUMER CREDIT ACT).

· If a builder or other jobbing workman calls at your door saying he's noticed you have slates loose on your roof or that your drive needs resurfacing, don't employ him. Ask a local firm to quote you a price for the work if, indeed, it really needs doing at all.

· If a doorstep seller won't leave when asked to then he or she is trespassing. You can use reasonable force to make them leave or you can call the police to evict them.

· Your rights to your money back (Sale of Goods Act) are just the same against a doorstep seller and their company as against a shopkeeper for goods bought in shops.

· Legal rights are fine of course but they don't help you to claim your money back if the seller doesn't leave a name or address or gives a false one. If you're planning to buy something expensive make sure you get the details of the company and check them out before parting with cash.

· Some firms who employ doorstep sellers are members of a trading association, the Direct Selling Association (DSA), 44 Russell Square, London WC1B 4JP. Under their code of practice members must guarantee everything they sell and give you 14 days to cancel your order. Only 30 or so companies currently belong to the DSA, but among them are some of the best known names in door-to-door selling including Avon Cosmetics and Tupperware. The DSA will also deal with complaints against members. If you've a complaint against a company which is not a member, tell your local trading standards or consumer protection office about them or, if someone is regularly operating a confidence trick in your area, ask your local paper to publish a warning to others.

See also: ARBITRATION, CODES OF PRACTICE, CONSUMER CREDIT ACT, COOLING-OFF PERIODS, TELEPHONE SELLING

Double Glazing

Double glazing is a costly item and although the majority of firms carrying out this work are reputable some have been guilty of high pressure sales and poor workmanship. As with any work you ask someone to carry out for you always get two or three different firms to give you a written quotation as to how much the job is going to cost. Discuss, in detail, the work to be carried out and if you need to have it finished by a certain date make this a part of the contract. Read the contract carefully taking special notice of prices, cancellation rights and any guarantees.

To help with some of the problems a code of practice has been established, agreed by the Glass and Glazing Federation (GGF), 44–48 Borough High Street, London SE1 1XB, 01-403 7177 and the Office of Fair Trading. The code covers all aspects of members' trading including advertising, selling, installation and quality standards.

If you sign the deal at home and are using credit then, under the Consumer Credit Act, you have a cooling-off period in which to change your mind (see CONSUMER CREDIT ACT). However, under the GGF code, you have the additional right to cancel the agreement even if you pay cash, so long as you sign the contract at your home or anywhere away from the trader's business premises and cancel within five days from the day you sign the contract. If you wish to cancel you must write to the address given in the contract.

If you're asked to pay a large deposit, query it. You could stand to lose your money if the firm goes bust and large companies shouldn't need more than a small goodwill payment, if anything at all. Under the code every GGF member has the deposit indemnity fund behind it which covers deposits of up to a quarter of the value of contracts worth up to £6,000. If, for example, the firm goes bust and doesn't finish the work, the GGF will arrange for another firm to complete it at a fair price minus the deposit. In some cases they will refund the deposit as an alternative.

Check with the firm that their windows comply with building regulations – this is your responsibility and not the firm's.

If you have a complaint take it up first with the firm who did the work. A letter often works better than a phone call but remember to keep a copy. If you're still not satisfied, and the firm is a member, write to the GGF. They will take up your complaint and try to reach a quick and satisfactory solution. They also offer a cheap, independent arbitration scheme. If the firm isn't a member and your local trading standards or consumer protection department can't help you may have to resort to taking the firm to court. Even if they are a member you could still sue them as an alternative to arbitration.

See also: ARBITRATION, CODES OF PRACTICE, CONSUMER CREDIT ACT, SERVICES

Dry Cleaning

If your dress goes into the dry cleaners a size 12 and comes out a size 8 what can you do about it, apart from scream? All too often we are made to feel as though *we've* been taken to the cleaners when dry cleaning goes wrong and the shop refuses to admit responsibility. But where do we stand legally?

As with all services, if a dry cleaner accepts your clothes it undertakes to carry out the cleaning with reasonable care, to a reasonable standard for a reasonable price (unless fixed, which it usually is) in a reasonable time (Supply of Goods and Services Act). If they don't do this, you can ask for your money back or get them to do the job again or, if the item is damaged permanently, demand compensation. Dry cleaning is a notoriously tricky area. There have been cases where some cleaners have tried to wriggle out of their responsibility by relying on exclusion clauses such as 'articles are left at owner's risk' or ones limiting the amount the firm will pay as compensation. But frankly these won't wash. Under the Unfair Contract Terms Act a cleaner can only rely on this type of statement if it is reasonable.

Three-quarters of launderers and dry cleaners in England, Scotland and Wales are members of the Association of British Laundry, Cleaning and Rental Services Ltd (ABLCRS), and, together with the Office of Fair

Trading, the Association has agreed a code of practice to which all members subscribe. The code doesn't, however, apply to launderettes and coin-operated dry cleaners.

Under the code members have agreed not to restrict their legal liability for negligence, for example not to set limits on the compensation they will pay. They agree to pay fair compensation if they destroy or damage an item or, where appropriate, pay for a repair. If the cleaning isn't satisfactory they will do it again.

If you need to complain, first give the firm involved the chance to put the matter right. If that fails you could ask your local trading standards department or consumer advice centre to mediate for you. They may suggest that you go back to the shop where you bought the item if the problem was due to a manufacturing fault. If the firm is a member of ABLCRS, you can ask their customer advisory service to help you solve the dispute. Their address is Customer Advisory Service, Association of British Laundry, Cleaning and Rental Services Ltd, Lancaster Gate House, 319 Pinner Road, Harrow, Middlesex HA1 4HX, 01-863 7755. The advisory service may suggest a laboratory test to help solve the problem. If so, and you and the firm both agree, they will arrange an independent test. You will have to pay a small fee which will be refunded if your claim is upheld. Some dry cleaners offer this anyway as part of their company policy for solving disputes. Even if the ABLCRS doesn't think a test necessary you can ask them to arrange one on your behalf. An ABLCRS member has to accept the findings of a test. Going to court is the final resort.

There are some things you can do to help avoid a dispute. For example, make sure you know what clothes are made of when you buy them. Look at the care labels in clothes (see CLOTHING). If in doubt, ask your dry cleaner if you should remove buttons or trimmings before cleaning or about any specialist cleaning that might be necessary.

See also: LAUNDRIES

Dutch Auction

A 'dutch auction' works the reverse way to a normal auction. Instead of the auctioneer selling to the highest bidder he sells to the lowest. The auctioneer starts at a high price and then comes down until someone bids. The skill in bidding at this type of auction is to keep your nerve and stay quiet until the very last minute to secure a bargain.

Duty Frees

Years ago death or deportation were the penalties for smuggling your way round excise duty. Today there's a much more pleasurable, and legal, way of avoiding it: international travel. Few of the 40 million arrivals at UK airports and sea terminals pass customs without some sort of duty-free purchases of which chief favourites are alcohol and tobacco.

If we really bought booze duty free, that is without excise duty and taxes, the price would drop by about 80 per cent instead of the mere 50 per cent which is usual, so the term duty 'free' is a bit of a misnomer.

During the last 20 years tax-free shopping has also become big business. Tax-free shops now rival high street stores in size, range of goods and image. At some outlets tax-free sales are outstripping the duty free takings. Tax, that is value added tax, applies to a wide range of goods including perfume, clothing, jewellery, electric and electronic goods, photographic equipment and gift items. Once again the goods may be a bargain but they are more 'tax-reduced' than 'tax-free'.

Here's a quick guide to your duty free allowances on coming into Britain. For what you can take from the UK into your holiday destination ask the duty free shop staff.

	Bought in ordinary shops and supermarkets in EEC	or	Bought in duty free shops or outside EEC
ALCOHOL			
Still table wine	5 litres	or	2 litres
Spirits	1.5 litres	or	1 litre
or			
Fortified wine	3 litres	or	2 litres
TOBACCO PRODUCTS			
Cigarettes	300	or	200
or			
Cigars	75	or	50
PERFUME	75 grammes (3 fl oz)	or	50 grammes (2 fl oz)
OTHER GOODS			
Gifts, etc, worth	£207	or	£28

E

'E' Numbers

Most packaged foods contain additives, among them preservatives to give them a longer shelf life or colourings to make them look more appealing. Manufacturers use about 3,500 additives. Some are found in nature, and are taken from plants, others are manufactured. All additives permitted for use in our foods have undergone stringent tests and are safe for most people although a few of us might have an allergic reaction to some, just as we do to certain foods.

Additives include preservatives, antioxidants, to stop fats and oils from going rancid, emulsifiers and stabilisers to help mix foods or stop them separating, colouring, flavour enhancers and sweeteners, anti-caking agents to stop lumps forming in powdery foods such as dried milk, and raising agents which act like baking powder to make food rise.

Of the permitted additives nearly 300 have been given a number, and when the additive has also been approved by the European Community the number has an 'E' in front of it. For example E110, found in some biscuits, is sunset yellow.

See also: FOOD LABELLING

Education

It is the duty of every parent to ensure that their child receives 'efficient full-time education suitable to his (or her) age, ability and aptitude, either by regular attendance at school or otherwise' according to the 1944 Education Act. Which, in simple terms, means that you don't have to send your child to school but you do have to show the local education authority (LEA) that he or she is being properly educated, even if it's at home. If you fail to show this, the LEA can serve a school attendance order on you and if need be take you to court to enforce it.

Formal education should begin from the start of the school term following the child's fifth birthday and continue until the child is at least 16.

While our education system is national it is administered locally by local education authorities whose duty it is to oversee the running of state schools. In London the Education Reform Bill has given individual boroughs the chance to take over responsibility for schools from the Inner London Education Authority in the future. If you have a complaint about your child's education, and the head can't or won't sort it out, you can complain to the school's board of governors – parents, teachers and local people are represented here. If that fails write to your local LEA direct. (In Scotland contact your local Director of Education.) You have a final right, in certain circumstances, to appeal to the Secretary of State for Education (or to the Secretary of State for Scotland or Northern Ireland).

If you do have a complaint the Advisory Centre for Education (ACE), 18 Victoria Park Square, London E2 9PB, 01-980 4596 gives free advice over the telephone on almost anything to do with state education, Monday to Friday 2–5 pm. You can also get a list of their useful publications by sending an s.a.e. The National Children's Bureau, 8 Wakley Street, London EC1V 7QE has lists of organisations concerned with all aspects of education both practical and campaigning. Education Otherwise is a self-help organisation which offers support and advice to families considering or practising alternative education for their children. You can write to Education Otherwise at 25 Common Lane, Hemmingford Abbotts, Cambridgeshire PE18 9AN, (0480) 63130.

Private schools are not part of the Local Education Authority's responsibility but they do have to be registered with the Department of Education and Science. The Independent Schools Information Service (ISIS) is at 56 Buckingham Gate, London SW1E 6AG, 01-630 8793.

For your rights over your child's education in school, see: SCHOOLS

Electricity
When dealing with any public service, be it for gas, telephone or electricity, keep a close eye on your bills – don't assume that they are correct and if you need to complain, persist. Keep all your bills. Write on

them when, where and how you paid, and if you have a query or can't afford to pay write to the Board's local office immediately. The Board will be sympathetic and may be able to suggest ways of paying which you can afford.

If you think you're going to have difficulty paying a big bill, ask about having a slot meter fitted so that you can pay as you go along. This can however be a serious security risk and if your meter is burgled you will still be expected to pay for the electricity used. A safer way is to save for bills by buying savings stamps from electricity showrooms and some post offices and then use them for your quarterly bill or you can ask about opening a monthly budget account. For this the Electricity Board works out what your annual electricity bill is likely to be and spreads it across 12 equal monthly payments. At the end of the year they then refund any money owing or adjust next year's payments if you owe them. In practice you'd be better putting the money into a building society account where it would be gaining interest until the bill falls due but this may not be so convenient. Households receiving Income Support may apply to the DHSS to have a sum of money paid direct to the Electricity Board each week and deducted from their benefit.

If you don't pay your bill the Electricity Board can disconnect you but to do so it has to comply with a strict code of practice laid down by the fuel industries and the Department of Energy. If you let the Board know of your difficulties they will not cut you off if you agree to an arrangement, to pay by instalments, and stick to it, even if it's only a few pounds a week. Nor will they cut off supply to a house where all the inhabitants are old age pensioners between 1 October and 31 March, nor if you owe the Board for something other than fuel, for example instalments on an electrical appliance. Full details of the code are available in a leaflet from your local showroom, and remember – keep the Board informed and they are less likely to cut you off!

If your bill is higher than you expected first check that you have not been sent an estimated reading because the meter reader couldn't get into your house. If this has happened you can fill in the correct figures and send back the bill. If not then the bill could be high because you've bought a new appliance, been in more than usual or had the heating turned on more often. If you think the bill is wrong you can ask the Board to check the reading. The phone number of your local Board is on the back of the bill, or call in your local showroom and ask them to send someone round. If you're still not satisfied you can ask the Department of Energy to send an inspector to check the meter for you. Their methods are very thorough and their verdict is legally binding. It might be advisable to pay part of the bill while this is being done just in case it is accurate, then you won't be faced with such a huge amount in the end.

If you buy your electricity from a landlord check how much you're paying. The Electricity Board sets a maximum price that landlords can charge tenants for fuel.

If you're not happy with the service of your local Electricity Board or the way you have been treated you should contact your Area Electricity Consultative Council (AECC), under 'E' in the phone book. They represent consumer interests and are independent of the Boards. If they can't resolve the problem the matter may be referred to the Electricity Council, the central body for the electricity supply industry in England and Wales. Alternatively, if your AECC thinks your complaint raises matters of wider national importance they can refer it to the Electricity Consumers' Council. Set up in 1977, it doesn't handle individual complaints but looks at wider matters such as energy conservation and price changes. Scotland and Northern Ireland have different procedures for dealing with complaints so check with your AECC or local Board.

See also: NATIONAL CONSUMER COUNCIL, RIGHTS OF ENTRY

Employment

Most of us need to go to work to clothe and feed ourselves and our families and while some of us are self-employed the majority work for someone else. Employment law has got more complex over the years but here's a brief guide to some of the more important points.

CONTRACT OF EMPLOYMENT: Once you have accepted an employer's offer of a job, a contract exists between the two of you. Within three months you should receive a copy of this in writing, setting out the terms of employment including any disciplinary or grievance procedures. It should also set out your hours of work, pay, holiday entitlement, sickness payments, pension scheme, length of notice required, job title and starting date.

PREGNANCY: Women who are pregnant have extra rights including the right to take time off to go to ante-natal care and the right to maternity leave and pay. Statutory maternity pay is paid for the first 18 weeks of absence due to pregnancy starting at or after the beginning of the 11th week before the expected birth: to qualify the woman has to have been employed continuously for at least 26 weeks before the beginning of the 14th week. The rules are quite complex as there are two rates, the 'higher' payable for only six weeks. For maternity leave she needs two years' continuous employment before the beginning of the 11th week. The employer must keep the woman's job open for her to return to up to 29 weeks after the child's birth, but he can ask her to confirm in writing that she intends to return. Some companies' schemes give benefits in addition to the statutory minimum.

TRADE UNIONS: You have a right not to be dismissed for belonging to a union and should be allowed reasonable time to carry out union duties. On the other hand, as long as no closed shop agreement operates, no employee can be dismissed for not belonging to a trade union.

UNFAIR DISMISSAL: A dismissal is only fair if the employee's behaviour warrants it, if he or she isn't capable or qualified for the job or if the employee is to be made redundant (see REDUNDANCY). It is unfair if the dismissal is because of racial or sexual discrimination. If you think you have been dismissed unfairly you can take your case to an industrial tribunal (see under I).

PART-TIME WORKERS: If you work part-time you are likely to have reduced rights. To get the benefits of the law you have to work at least 16 hours a week, or eight hours a week if you've been in the job for five years.

Environmental Health Department

If you find a cockroach in your takeaway hamburger, a slug in your bottle of ginger beer or a fly in your soup you should report it to your local Environmental Health Department (number under your local authority in the phone book). They are responsible for enforcing criminal legislation relating to food, hygiene and other public health and housing matters.

Under the Food and Drugs Act it's against the law to sell food or drink which is unfit for human consumption. There are also strict regulations about food hygiene including cleanliness in factories and shops, restaurants and cafés, anywhere food is sold. It also covers ice-cream vans and mobile food stalls.

If you think someone has broken the law you should report it to the

Environmental Health Department who will then visit the factory, restaurant or shop in question and investigate. If they find there's imminent risk to health they have the power to close down premises within 3 days.

Don't delay in reporting to the department. For example, if you've bought mouldy food try to do it the same day so that you can show the state of the food when you bought it. If a trader is prosecuted for breaking the Act he can be fined or, in the case of a restaurant, could lose his licence. You might also be entitled to compensation.

See also: FOOD

Equal Opportunities

It's been more than ten years since the Equal Pay (EPA) and Sex Discrimination Acts (SDA) came into force and began the sexual and economic revolution that gives women equality with men in employment, pay, education and money matters including buying a house. The aim of the EPA is to get rid of discrimination between men and women in basic rates of pay and other conditions of employment. Under it you can claim equal pay if you do the same, or broadly similar, work; if your job has been rated equal to a man's under a job evaluation scheme; or if your job is of 'equal value' to a man's. To check whether your job is of 'equal value' start by asking yourself if a man doing your job would be satisfied with your rate of pay. Then, if you can, find someone who is being paid what you think you're worth, by the same employer, and base your claim on comparing your job with his. Compare your skills, the responsibilities involved, the effort required and the conditions in which the jobs are done. While you don't have to show that you could do his job you do have to show that as a whole the two jobs are of equal merit. If you think you have a good case for equal pay your claim should be made to an industrial tribunal. Apply while in the job or within six months of leaving. You can get the relevant form from your union, local employment office or by asking at the Citizens Advice Bureau. Both the EPA and SDA apply equally to men and women but in practice most of the discrimination has been against women.

For further help or advice on equal pay or any other form of discrimination at work or in general you should write to the Equal Opportunities Commission (head office), Overseas House, Quay Street, Manchester M3 3HN, 061-833 9244 or to regional offices at Caerwys House, Windsor Place, Cardiff CF1 1LB and St Andrew's House, 141

West Nile Street, Glasgow GW1 2RN. They not only have useful leaflets but in some cases, where a general principle is involved, will help take a case to court.

See also: DISCRIMINATION

Estate Agents

Anyone can set up as an estate agent. They are controlled by the Estate Agents Act 1979 and complaints which cannot be sorted out should be made to the local authority trading standards or consumer protection department. According to a national survey conducted by the Consumers' Association, half the people who use an estate agent each year are not happy with the service. High fees and inefficiency are the main grumbles.

So, what should you look for if you need an estate agent?

IF SELLING: Shop around, compare prices, services and facilities. Fees can vary according to area and to the agreement you strike. For example, if you agree to giving one firm sole agency they might charge you a lower percentage than if you put your house in the hands of more than one estate agent. (Their fees are based on a percentage of the price the property is sold for.) However it's not wise to give the estate agent sole selling rights, as opposed to sole agency, as this way you could end up paying the percentage even if you sell the property yourself! According to the Consumers' Association, it's best to agree only to a 'no sale, no fee' arrangement.

IF BUYING: Check the details of the property carefully – an estate agent's description is not bound by the Trade Descriptions Act.

Some agents are members of professional bodies who will look into complaints against members if you can't resolve them yourself. They can then fine, warn, suspend or even expel a member from the Association and in extreme cases the Office of Fair Trading, Field House, 15–25 Breams Buildings, London EC4A 1PR, 01-242 2858, can take action against an agent.

Useful addresses of associations:
Royal Institution of Chartered Surveyors (RICS), 12 Great George Street, London SW1P 3AD for agents who are also qualified surveyors.

Incorporated Society of Valuers and Auctioneers, 3 Cadogan Gate, London SW1X 0AS.
National Association of Estate Agents, Arbon House, 21 Jury Street, Warwick CV34 4EH.

The advantages of using an estate agent who is a member of one of these associations is that they have schemes to protect you from losing money, including deposits on a property you intend to buy, and have rules of conduct plus a complaints procedure. It's worth remembering, however, that you don't have to put down a deposit when buying a house – it's only a gesture of goodwill on your part. In Scotland deposits are actually banned and other aspects of house buying are also different. If you are in any doubt about the procedure consult a solicitor or your local Citizens Advice Bureau.

See also: PROPERTY SHOPS, SURVEYORS

Estimates

If you've ever been given an 'estimate' as to how much a job will cost only to find that the figure has doubled by the time the bill arrives then the chances are you've been caught out by the old estimate versus quotation trick. Although neither has any firm basis in law, in general an estimate is only a rough idea of what a job will cost, while a quotation usually indicates a firm price. But, to be really sure, agree in writing a fixed price for the job to be undertaken and then that can only be deviated from if the job changes in a material way. And don't forget if you do get a written estimate or quotation, to check how long it is good for. It's unreasonable to suppose a price today will be valid in six months' time.

See also: QUOTATIONS, SERVICES

Exchanging Goods

If you buy something and take it home only to find it's the wrong size, the wrong colour or that you plain don't like it then you have no right in law to have it exchanged. Although some shops, if you keep your receipt, will do this as a matter of goodwill.

Own branding of goods, particularly own-label clothes, has made identification easier and you should be able to take goods back to any branch of a large chain – though watch out for franchises like Benetton which look like a chain but aren't. A word of warning too on pre-packed items: a shop's willingness to refund or exchange will depend on their ability to re-sell the unwanted item, so if it comes in special packaging, for example a bubble pack, don't break it or you could be stuck with the goods inside.

Of course, if the goods are faulty or the shop breaks the contract in some other way, you should get a full refund.

Exclusion Clauses

An exclusion clause, or disclaimer, is a crafty device some traders use to try to deny the consumer his or her legal rights. The most common are found in notices in shops, restaurants and public places. For example, in a car park it could say 'Cars are left at owner's risk' or in a restaurant cloakroom 'We accept no responsibility for articles left here.' They are also common in the small print of manufacturers' guarantees and in contracts for goods and services.

Thanks to the Unfair Contract Terms Act some exclusion clauses have no effect while others are only valid if the trader can prove in court that they are reasonable in the circumstances. The Act has meant that really nasty disclaimers, like those restricting responsibility for death or injury, have disappeared. Some like those found in the small print of contracts or booking conditions might be considered reasonable, others are 'try-ons' intended to deter you from pursuing your legal rights. Under the Act exclusion clauses are not valid if they try to limit a company's liability for death or injury caused by their negligence. Similarly clauses which try to restrict a trader's responsibility for loss or damage to your property caused by his negligence are only valid if they are reasonable and that depends on the circumstances of each case. And if you didn't know about the clause before you made the contract then the company can't rely on it however reasonable it is. So, if a cleaner ruins your leather jacket he must not then produce 'terms and conditions' which try to limit the amount of compensation payable. No clause which tries to take away our rights under the Sale of Goods Act is valid, e.g. 'Sale goods may not be returned'.

As a general rule, if you come up against an exclusion clause press on with your claim as if the clause weren't there. If the company wants to rely on it, it is up to them to prove that the exclusion is fair and reasonable.

See also: HOLIDAYS, SALE OF GOODS ACT

F

Fake Goods
See: COUNTERFEITING

Faulty Goods

If you buy something that is faulty, whether it's a piece of rancid cheese or a silent stereo unit, then under the Sale of Goods Act you are entitled to your money back. You do not have to accept a repair or a replacement. If you accept a repair then make sure you tell the seller, preferably in writing, that you do so out of goodwill but reserve the right to a refund if you are not satisfied with the repair.

Remember that your rights, at all times, are with the shop or seller and not with the manufacturers, so don't be fobbed off with 'I'll send it back to the manufacturer for you, madam.' Let them do that, by all means, but get your money back first. If you do let them send it back, for example if it's the last pair of shoes in that style in the shop and the assistant tells you the manufacturer may be able to put it right, then once again make it clear that you may still claim your refund at a later date.

The Sale of Goods Act entitles you to your money back if the goods are not of merchantable quality, not fit for their purpose or not as described. For example, a chair with a broken spindle is not of merchantable quality, if it loses a leg it's not fit for its purpose and if it turns out to be red when on the box it said it was black then it's not as described.

You can't claim your money back if you knew about the fault before you bought the goods or if you examined the items and should have noticed the defect (you don't have to examine them).

See also: GOODS, SALE OF GOODS ACT

Fences

If you are in dispute with your neighbour about where to fence the boundary of your property, look at the title deeds. They may contain plans showing the boundary and even information about whose responsibility it is to maintain the fence or hedge. If you haven't a copy yourself, you might find them with the solicitor who acted for you in the purchase of the property, with your mortgage lender or with the Land Registry, if the land is registered. You can check whether your property is registered by telephoning your district Land Registry (in phone book or via London headquarters) or in Scotland the Register of Sasines, Meadowbank House, 153 London Road, Edinburgh EH8 7AU. Many boundary hedges and fences don't actually run exactly along the 'legal' boundaries but if they are well established you may have to accept the situation, and anyway it isn't worth worrying about if you and your neighbour are both happy with the situation.

There is no general duty to put up a fence on your boundary nor to maintain one, although this may be a stipulation in your lease or title deeds. And if, for example, you keep an animal you would have a duty to take reasonable steps to ensure that it did not escape and cause damage to another person or property.

See also: ANIMALS

Film Services

There are few things more frustrating and disappointing than taking photographs of a happy holiday or a memorable family occasion only to find that the film processing service loses your film or, as happened to a friend, sends you someone else's bouncing baby shots instead of your own.

If a firm loses your film you might be entitled to compensation as well as a new film and free processing, particularly if you can show that the lost film was of special significance, for example, a silver wedding celebration or your first trip to the United States.

If you get your prints but they turn out to be of poor quality, don't be afraid to go back and ask for them to be done again free of charge. It might be that the negatives were poor or it could be that the processing went wrong.

To try to help overcome some of these problems the photographic trade associations have prepared a code of practice, Photocode, with the help of the Office of Fair Trading. Photocode covers buying a film, having it processed and even buying photographic equipment. If you're in dispute with a company which is a Photocode member, you can ask their trade association to help settle the dispute. Photocode also has a low cost arbitration scheme. The main organisation representing film processors, a Photocode member, is the Association of Photographic Laboratories, 9 Warwick Court, Grays Inn, London WC1R 5DJ, 01-405 2762.

See also: ARBITRATION, CODES OF PRACTICE

Finance Companies

You will often see adverts in newspapers and magazines by finance companies offering loans. They can be useful if you're having trouble getting credit or want one loan to pay off a series of smaller debts. Many of them are subsidiaries of one of the big UK or foreign banks and also offer investment schemes. But be careful, watch out for the high rates of interest some finance companies charge. Check the APR (see CREDIT).

If you have a problem with a finance company or want more information write to the Finance Houses Association, 18 Upper Grosvenor Street, London W1X 9PB.

Financial Services Act

How do you know that the financial advice you're getting is the best available? Until recently the answer to that often-asked question was 'you don't'. While for years financial advisers, be they banks, building societies or insurance companies, have happily handed out armfuls of figures and forecasts for our financial futures, until recently there was no guarantee that you were getting independent advice never mind the best available.

Now, thanks to the Financial Services Act 1986, which came fully into operation early in 1988 investment advisers have to be authorised and run their business according to strict guidelines. They must also give the 'best' advice taking into account each individual's needs and circumstances. If you are not satisfied with the advice you get you can complain through the appropriate adviser's regulatory body, for example, the Financial Intermediaries, Managers, Brokers Regulatory Association (FIMBRA).

The Act covers life assurance, pensions, unit trusts and shares, among others, but not loans (including mortgages). The Department of Trade and Industry has set up the Securities Investment Board (SIB), 3 Royal

Exchange Buildings, London EC3V 3NL, to act as a watchdog for the
Act. They too will look into complaints as well as giving you the name of
the appropriate regulatory body for the type of adviser involved.

Fireworks
Over the years firework manufacturers have taken voluntary steps to
improve firework safety, for example by selling mostly boxed collections
and by reducing the explosive content of bangers. The Government has
also played its part by banning the sale of fireworks to under 16s and
making it an offence to throw a firework in the street or in a public place.

If you're planning a bonfire party remember the Firework Code:
· Keep fireworks in a closed box – take them out one at a time and put
  the top back on at once.
· Follow the instructions carefully – read them by torchlight, never by
  naked flame.
· Light end of firework fuse at arm's length – preferably with a safety
  firework lighter or fuse wick.
· Never return to a firework once lit – it may go off in your face.
· Never throw fireworks.
· Never put fireworks in your pocket.
· Keep pets indoors.
· Never fool with fireworks.

Fixed Fee Interview
This is a cheap form of legal advice. For only £5 you can have 30 minutes
of discussion and advice with a solicitor – a fraction of the normal cost of
a solicitor's services. It isn't means tested so anyone can use the service.
Check with your local Citizens Advice Bureau or the Law Society, 113
Chancery Lane, London WC2A 1PL, 01-242 1222, for a list of solicitors
in your area who take part in the scheme – not all do. A similar service is
called the advice and assistance scheme (see GREEN FORM SCHEME).
     See also: LEGAL AID

Food Labelling
If you've been reading the label on your sauce bottle recently you've
probably noticed it's been getting longer. Food labelling regulations help
control the quality of pre-packed food and, by giving us more information, help us to decide what to buy. Some foods, for example chocolate
products, milk, coffee and wine, have special labelling rules while the

rest have to be marked with the following: the name of the food; list of ingredients in descending order of weight; any additives such as flavour enhancers, preservatives or colouring; datemark or 'best before' date stamp; and the name and business address of the manufacturer, packer or seller.

It is not illegal to sell food after its datemark has expired so long as it is still fit for human consumption. Non-pre-packed food must be marked with the name of the product, eg the variety if potatoes, list any additives and sometimes give the country of origin.

Today you might also find labels giving nutritional information. These include fibre, sugar, salt, fat, carbohydrate and calorie contents.

If you have a complaint about a food label, first take it up with the manufacturer or shop where you bought it. If you're still not satisfied, contact your local authority trading standards or consumer protection department; they are responsible for enforcing the law on food labelling.

See also: 'E' NUMBERS

Footwear

Footwear is a particularly tricky area for consumers, with the official life expectancy of a shoe being much shorter than most of us would imagine. However, as a simple guideline a high-fashion shoe shouldn't be expected to stand up to a tramp across the moors or even, probably, to heavy day-to-day wear, while a stout brogue should. Similarly, while a heel shouldn't drop off a pair of court shoes within a few weeks of buying them, you wouldn't be able to complain if you'd been driving in them.

If you have a complaint about your shoes, return them to the shop or any branch of the chain of shops where you bought them and complain to the shop manager. If he or she agrees that your complaint is justified then you should get your money back or at least some of it – how much depends on the type of fault and how long you have had the shoes. If the manager disagrees, he may offer to send them back to the manufacturer – you don't have to agree to this – or to the shop's head office for an expert opinion. As an alternative you could ask your local consumer advice centre or trading standards (consumer protection) department for help in settling the matter or ask for the shoes to be sent to the Footwear Testing Centre for an independent report. You may have to pay the postage and a fee for this but if your complaint is upheld the shop should reimburse you. If they refuse to accept the Centre's findings, you've probably got a good enough case to go to the small claims court (or summary cause procedure) for compensation – but it might be worth seeking legal advice first.

One way of being sure of good service is to buy shoes at a shop which honours the footwear code of practice. The code is backed by the industry's main trade associations and covers shoe shops and repairers. It tries to ensure that complaints are handled with minimum fuss, and if you have to have shoes tested at the Footwear Testing Centre shops who honour the code pay two-thirds of the fee while you pay one-third. If you win, the retailer refunds your third and must abide by the findings of the Centre.

Under the Sale of Goods Act, goods, including shoes, must be of merchantable quality (tassels should not drop off loafers), be fit for their purpose (the heel shouldn't drop off when you walk on it) and be as described (a shoe described as waterproof should be).

Here are some common situations to consider:
· Don't be fobbed off by a salesman who says all he can do is send the shoes back to the manufacturer. Your contract is with him and he should put the matter right.
· If you find the shoes, when you get them home, are the wrong colour for that special outfit then tough luck. Some shops might exchange them for you as an act of goodwill but you can't demand it.
· Don't be fobbed off with a credit note unless you really do want another pair of shoes from that shop – for example, if you are waiting for your size of a particular pair to come in. Once you've accepted a credit note it can be difficult to get your money back later if you don't find anything you want.
· My boots let water in! This is a common complaint but the sad truth is that 'fashion' shoes or boots aren't usually suitable for British winters. If you have a particular use for the shoes in mind, eg long walks or wading through farmyards, tell the shopkeeper and let him advise you what is suitable. Many disputes arise over what is reasonable wear for a shoe and generally it is considered unreasonable to expect a high-fashion shoe to stand up to a lot of walking or disco dancing.
· If a shoe is falsely described to you, for example you are told it is leather when the material is manmade, then not only could you claim your money back under the Sale of Goods Act, but also the trader might be liable to prosecution under the Trade Descriptions Act.

Friendly Societies

Dating back to the 17th century, friendly societies were formed from groups of friends and neighbours who met in houses and inns to provide money for sickness, retirement and funeral expenses. They dwindled in popularity earlier this century, but are now coming back into fashion offering longer term, tax-free savings. To save with a friendly society you usually have to be married or bringing up a dependent child or children. Most schemes are designed to last for 10 years and you could lose out if you cash in early. While your investment is tax-free you have to pay a service charge to the society for handling it for you.

Fuel

See: COAL, ELECTRICITY, GAS

Funerals

Having to make funeral arrangements is a difficult enough task without suffering at the hands of an unscrupulous funeral director. So, play safe and choose one who is a member of the National Association of Funeral Directors, 57 Doughty Street, London WC1N 2NE, 01-242 9388. The Association has a code of practice, backed by the Office of Fair Trading, covering all services provided by members except the supply of gravestones. Complaints about a member of the Association that can't be resolved between you can be referred to the Association for conciliation and, if that fails, arbitration. But take legal advice if it gets this far, as you can't use the arbitration scheme *and* take the director to court. You have to pay a small fee for arbitration – refundable if you win.

In law the service of a funeral director should be reasonable under the Supply of Goods and Services Act (see SERVICES).

See: DEATH

Furniture

Under the Sale of Goods Act, if you buy furniture which is faulty or defective in some way you may be entitled to all or part of your money back from the shop where you bought it. How much you're entitled to will depend on a number of factors, including the seriousness of the fault, how long you've had the furniture, how much longer it could be expected to last and how much you paid for it. If the shop or the manufacturer is a member of a furniture trade association then you will have further rights in addition to your basic legal ones. The National

Association of Retail Furnishers, 17–21 George Street, Croydon CR9 1QT, 01-680 8444 has agreed to abide by a code of practice in association with the Office of Fair Trading. The code covers advertising, labelling, delivery, price, repairs and complaints.

If you have a complaint about an item of furniture first take it up with the shop where you bought it. If that fails see if your local trading standards department or consumer advice centre can help. If you're still not satisfied, and the retailer is a member of a trade association, ask their help. They will try to settle the matter between you and, if necessary, can ask an independent examiner to inspect the furniture and report on its condition. You would have to pay a small fee for this which would be refunded if your complaint is upheld. Finally, the association can refer your case to arbitration, for a fee once again refundable if you win, under the code. If you choose arbitration you forfeit the right to take the case to court so seek legal advice on which course to take.

Furniture is also covered by safety regulations which at present say that most new, upholstered furniture must carry warning labels if tests show it could catch fire from a lighted cigarette or match, while from 1989 the most dangerous foam materials will be banned from new furniture altogether. If you don't see a label, be on the safe side and check with the salesman.

See also: DELIVERY DATES, SALE OF GOODS ACT

G

Garage Sales

Garage sales are an increasingly popular way of getting rid of your
unwanted rubbish. After all, your junk could be someone else's jewel. If
you're thinking of holding one, get together with your neighbours or
friends living locally to make it really worthwhile. So long as the sale is a
one-off private affair, and not a business in disguise, it's perfectly legal. If
you buy goods from such a sale then you have no rights under the Sale of
Goods Act if they prove faulty.

See also: SALE OF GOODS ACT (private sales), SECONDHAND GOODS

Gardens

What you do in your own back garden is your own business – up to a
point. But let the thistles get out of hand or install a new gate and you
could be in trouble with the law. Here's a breakdown on some of the
things you can and can't do:

YOU CAN:
· Secure your garden with an electric fence or by putting broken glass on
  the top of a wall. But, you could be liable for an injury caused by it –
  even an intruder could sue you if they cut themselves on the glass. An
  electric fence must have warning tags unless the land on both sides of it
  is your own private ground.
· Light a bonfire or barbecue. Smoke from these only becomes a
  nuisance, in the eyes of the law, if it is continuous or repeated. If smoke
  from your neighbour's garden is a regular occurrence you should
  complain to your local environmental health department.
· Keep a compost heap as long as it is properly looked after.

· Play loud music. One afternoon's disturbance will not bring official-
dom down on you but repeated or continuous loud music can be
reported to the environmental health department who will then
investigate. If next door are still partying at 3 am, a friendly word from
the local police may help to quieten them!
· Lop off overhanging branches from a neighbour's trees – but you
should hand them back to him. In law they are still his property. If the
tree itself is spoiling your view or keeping the sun off your plants
there's little you can do apart from asking your neighbour politely for
his co-operation in cutting it back.
· Let your cat do what it likes. The law says you can claim compensation if straying horses, cattle or sheep make a mess on your land, but
dogs and cats are exempt.
· Grow weeds so long as they don't get in anyone's way. Certain
varieties like thistles, docks and ragworts are regarded as 'injurious'
because they can ruin farmers' crops and if you allow these to run riot
you could fall foul of the Weeds Act.

YOU CAN'T:
· Keep next door's child's ball if it comes into your garden. Although
they have no right to come and retrieve it, it is still their property so all
you can do is leave it where it drops – or throw it back.
· Dig up plants in the garden or growing up walls when you are moving
house. They have become 'fixtures' and so part of the property. If you
can't bear to move without a prized bush, then technically you should
have your solicitor write it into your contract as part of the deal.
· Put up a gate or fence more than one metre in height in front of your
own property (two metres anywhere else) without first getting planning permission from the local authority. But you can grow a hedge as
high as you like. The size of trees, shrubs and bushes is not subject to
planning control but you should check with your local authority
before you cut a big tree down.
· Stop someone parking outside your home. If someone blocks your
drive, the best you can do is leave a nasty note. A no parking sign has
no legal backing, unless of course it is a police notice!

It is your duty to take reasonable care to protect visitors on your
property, even unwanted ones, from unexpected hazards. For example
if you leave a ladder around and a child climbs it and hurts itself you

could be held liable, but it would be reasonable to assume that an adult knows the risks of climbing ladders and they couldn't therefore blame you if they fell – unless the ladder is defective. Scaffolding could be subject to local rules so check with the local council before you put this up.

See also: ANIMALS, INSURANCE, NEIGHBOURS

Gas

If you have dispute over your bill or other problems with your gas supply first tackle your local gas region, under G in the phone book or look for their address on the back of your bill. British Gas is divided into 12 regions including Scotland and Wales. If you're still not satisfied, the Gas Consumers' Council may be able to help. The Council is a watchdog body for the industry but totally independent from it. There are 12 offices, one for each region, and they will look into problems concerning your gas supply, cooker, fire or central heating appliance, their installation or other service you need to keep them going, including spare parts, repairs and safety checks. They can also take up individual cases with companies or the relevant gas region on your behalf. Your local Council's address and phone number should also be in the phone book under Gas, on the back of your gas bill or check with your nearest Citizens Advice Bureau.

Gifts

If you've been given something as a present which turns out to be faulty then you should ask the person who gave it to you to take it back to the shop where he or she bought it and ask for their money back. Under the

Sale of Goods Act only the buyer has this right against the shop. In practice, however, if you have the receipt from the buyer, the shop isn't likely to know the difference let alone dispute the matter on these grounds. On the other hand, if you just don't want the present you're not entitled to your money back although, in practice, many shops will give you a credit note or swap the item for you. If you're buying a present for someone and you're not quite sure about it, it's a good idea to ask the shop at the time what they're prepared to do if you should want to bring it back.

See also: SALE OF GOODS ACT

Gold
See: HALLMARKS

Goods
SAFETY: There is now greater protection for the consumer against dangerous goods than ever before. If you are injured because of a defect in something you buy you can claim against the manufacturer under the Consumer Protection Act 1987 which came into force at the beginning of 1988. This Act also places a general duty on all people who supply goods, be they manufacturer or retailer, to make sure they are safe, although a retailer has a defence if he didn't know nor had reasonable grounds for believing that the item failed to comply with the general safety requirement.

This new Act is designed to cover goods not previously covered by safety standards or regulations but does not extend to secondhand goods.

Many products are already covered by special safety requirements (see BRITISH STANDARDS INSTITUTION, BSI) and the sale of others is restricted by law, for example cigarettes, fireworks and medicines.

FAULTY: Under the Sale of Goods Act you are entitled to your money back, from the shop where you bought the goods, if they are not of merchantable quality, fit for their purpose or as described (see SALE OF GOODS ACT).

MAIL ORDER: If goods bought by mail order are faulty or dangerous your rights are exactly the same as if you went into a shop to buy them (see above). If you have any other complaint about a mail order company then write to the customer liaison department of the company. If you bought through an advertisement in a newspaper or magazine (not a classified ad), you should also write to the advertising manager of the publication under the Mail Order Protection Scheme (SEE MAIL ORDER). It is important to keep a record of all orders and goods or money sent when dealing with mail order companies.

SECONDHAND: If you buy secondhand goods from a shop or a dealer you are protected by the Sale of Goods Act but you can't expect something secondhand to be as good as new, so if the goods are faulty what you can expect could depend on how old they are and what you paid for them. If you buy privately you have little protection. For example, a secondhand Ford Fiesta bought from an individual has only to be as described. It needn't be either of merchantable quality nor fit for its purpose. (See also SALE OF GOODS ACT and SECONDHAND GOODS)

UNSOLICITED: If you receive unsolicited goods, such as encyclopaedias on the doormat, you should take care of them until they legally become yours. They are yours 30 days from the day you tell the sender to collect them or, if you do nothing, in 6 months. (See INERTIA SELLING, UNSOLICITED GOODS).

See also: BARGAINS, CARS, CHANGING GOODS, COMPLAINING, COUNTERFEITING, DANGEROUS GOODS, FAULTY GOODS, GIFTS, MAIL ORDER, MERCHANTABLE QUALITY, SALE OF GOODS ACT, SALES, SECONDHAND GOODS

Green Form Scheme

Properly named the legal advice and assistance scheme but commonly nicknamed after the colour of the application form this is a cheap kind of legal advice available to people with a low income and few savings. A solicitor will be able to tell you by doing a few sums whether or not you're likely to qualify. If you do then the scheme covers most common legal problems including divorce, maintenance wrangles, accidents, housing problems and making a will. Under the green form scheme a solicitor can give you advice, write letters for you and prepare a written case for a tribunal hearing. He can also take advice from a barrister on your behalf. But he can't actually represent you in court apart from a few exceptions such as maintenance and custody hearings. For more costly legal problems you would have to apply for legal aid as the sums involved under the green form scheme are quite small. For more details on the green form scheme ask at your local Citizens Advice Bureau or write to the Law Society, 113 Chancery Lane, London WC2A 1PL, 01-242 1222. A similar scheme operates in Scotland, but the form is pink!

See also: FIXED FEE INTERVIEW, LEGAL AID, SOLICITORS

Guarantees

At best a manufacturer's guarantee will mean a free repair when something goes wrong. But at its worst a guarantee is simply not worth the paper it's written on. Guarantees and extended warranties, which protect you after the guarantee has run out, are now available for many products and services, from electrical goods to major building work. But there is growing concern that they are not always such a boon to consumers as the suppliers would have us believe. And according to the Office of Fair Trading, one in five people making a claim under a guarantee is dissatisfied with the outcome.

A guarantee cannot take away your legal rights under the Sale of Goods Act. It is in addition to these rights and cannot alter them. If something goes wrong with goods you buy, or with a service, and it's still under guarantee then you have to decide whether you want to claim from the manufacturer under the guarantee or go back to the shop or trader and claim against him. Before deciding, read the small print of the guarantee. Do you have to pay postage? Does it cover both parts and labour? Do you want a repair, replacement or refund? Usually a guarantee will only provide one of the first two. Be careful, it can be difficult, although not impossible, to get your money back from the seller once you've accepted a repair under guarantee.

Sometimes the manufacturer will ask you to send back a registration card after buying goods. If you don't, then in theory he could refuse to honour the guarantee. In practice he's unlikely to if you have proof of date of purchase.

When it comes to services, if you've having any major work done like home improvement work, play safe and choose a firm which is a member of a trade association who will honour any guarantee that firm gives should it go bust.

See also: MAINTENANCE CONTRACTS, SALE OF GOODS ACT, SERVICES, WARRANTIES

H

Hairdressers

Talk to any woman about her hairdresser and she's likely to recall the time the stylist cut too much off, the perm fell out after only a week or she looked so awful she had to wear a wig. Hairdressers can make or ruin our looks. Anyone can set up as a hairdresser. They don't need to be qualified or even trained. If they are trained to an approved standard, normally a two-year full-time college course, they can register with the Hairdressing Council. Only one in three hairdressers is in fact registered and even those that aren't checked by the Council. Members do, however, have to conform to health and safety regulations. The only real power of the Council is to take someone off the register if there are serious complaints about a member – but this doesn't, of course, stop the hairdresser continuing trading.

If you're unhappy with the way your hairdresser has done your hair, complain as soon as you can – if possible before you pay. If it isn't something that can be put right immediately ask the salon manager for a price reduction or a free hairdo at a later date. If you want to claim compensation, for example if the junior carelessly splashes your clothes with bleach or your skin reacts after a perm, you will have to show that the hairdresser didn't act as a reasonably competent hairdresser would have done in the circumstances. If the damage is physical – for instance a skin rash – you'll need photographic evidence and a medical opinion from your doctor in case you have to pursue the case in court. If you can show you've suffered at the hairdresser's hands you can claim a refund, the cost of getting your hair back to a reasonable condition, any extra expenses incurred such as fares to and from the salon as well as possible compensation for pain and suffering.

The amount a court will award for distress or damage will very much

depend on the damage or psychological harm that the hairdresser
has caused. For instance, a model who relies on her looks for work
would be awarded a higher amount because her appearance is important in her work.

If your clothes are damaged you should claim either the cost of dry
cleaning or all or part of the cost of replacing the garment – how much
will depend on its age and the extent of the damage.

The Hairdressing Council, 12 David House, 45 High Street, South
Norwood, London SE25 6HJ, will give advice and help you with complaints against members. If all else fails you could take your case to the
small claims court at the county court.

See: SERVICES

Hallmarks

Articles made of gold, silver or platinum are given a hallmark by the
assay offices to show their quality and authenticity. Anything which is
not hallmarked must carry the description 'rolled' or 'plated', as in
'rolled gold' and 'silver plate'. There are a few exceptions, for example
some items are too small or too thin to be hallmarked. Hallmarking dates
back to 1300 but today is governed by the Hallmarking Act 1973 and
passing off an item as a precious metal or counterfeiting or altering a
hallmark can lead to a prison sentence. Shops may label something
'gold' or 'silver' referring to its colour but the distinction must be made
clear, and anyone trading in precious metals has to display a notice
issued by the British Hallmarking Council explaining the system.

If you want further information write to the British Hallmarking
Council, St Philips House, St Philips Place, Birmingham B3 2PP.

Health Council (Scotland)

See: COMMUNITY HEALTH

Health Service

If you want to complain about the NHS – either something they've done
or something they've failed to do – then here's how. Complaints about
poor service by a GP, dentist, pharmacist or optician – and this would
include anything from a rude receptionist to the actual treatment you
receive – should be made to your local Family Practitioner Committee
(under F in the phone book) in England and Wales, the Secretary of the
Health Board in Scotland and the Chief Administrative Officer of the
local Health and Central Services Agency in Northern Ireland. You

should complain within a few weeks of the incident. As a result of this the practitioner can be reported to their disciplinary body and you could be reimbursed the cost of any additional treatment that has been necessary to put the matter right. If you want compensation you would have to go to court.

Complaints about hospital organisation or poor medical treatment in hospital should be made to the person responsible. If that fails, then write to the appropriate senior member of staff such as the consultant, chief nursing officer or hospital administrator. If you're still not satisfied the area health authority (Health Board) will consider complaints about organisation and the regional Medical Officer about treatment.

There are also Health Service Ombudsmen who will investigate complaints about health service administration, but not about treatment. For example, he will look into delays in admission, loss of a patient's property or lack of information being given to patients or relatives. He cannot look into problems connected with diagnosis or the clinical judgement of medical staff. His address is the Parliamentary Commissioner and Health Service Ombudsman, Church House, Great Smith Street, London SW1, 01-212 7676 or see under NORTHERN IRELAND, SCOTLAND and WALES.

For initial help with any complaint, including how best to present your case, contact your Local or Community Health Council (CHC) under C or H in the phone book (in Northern Ireland it's the District Committee). They represent consumers' interests in the NHS and will advise you about your rights. The CHC also has information on the Health Service Ombudsman.

See also: DENTISTS, DOCTORS, HOSPITALS, OPTICIANS, PHARMACISTS

Hire

At some time in our lives most of us hire something, whether it's a car for a weekend, a van to move house or a shampooer to clean the carpets. Legally the hired item still belongs to the person who hired it out and you have to take reasonable care of it and could be forced to pay compensation if it is damaged. Hired goods, like those you buy, must be of merchantable quality, as described and fit for their purpose. If they aren't you can cancel the agreement under the Supply of Goods and Services Act.

Hire agreements, like credit agreements, may be regulated by the Consumer Credit Act.

Hire Purchase

Hire purchase is where you pay for goods, usually a specific item, by regular instalments. You generally have to pay a deposit to enable you to take the items home. The HP agreement must show the cash price, the total hire purchase price and the amount of each instalment. You don't own the goods until you've paid off the final instalment and so must take reasonable care of them and not sell them to anyone else. However, once you have paid a third of the total price the trader or finance company can't repossess the goods without a court order.

HP agreements are now strictly controlled by the Consumer Credit Act which sets rules for advertising, information about interest rates, cancellation of agreements and what a trader can do if you default on a payment. If you default, then to recover the goods or arrears the trader or finance company must serve a default notice on you outlining your breach of contract and giving you at least seven days to put it right. In practice, if you fall behind on HP payments, keep the trader or finance company informed by offering to pay something, however small, on a regular basis. This usually stops any action; after all, all they want is their money.

See also: CONSUMER CREDIT ACT, COOLING-OFF PERIOD

Holiday Insurance

If you're going on holiday abroad it is vital to have adequate holiday insurance to cover cancellation, airport delays, any medical treatment you might need and loss of or damage to your luggage. You might also want to consider cancellation insurance for a holiday in Britain. The easiest way to buy holiday insurance is through your tour company but it's always worth checking in the brochure what is covered as you might get a better deal by taking out independent cover. Most travel insurance policies are inclusive packages and include: cancellation, if you have to cancel a booking through circumstances beyond your control, for example if you or your travelling companion are taken ill; curtailment, where through illness or death of a loved one you have to come home early; medical expenses abroad; personal accident cover if you die or lose a limb; personal liability cover for if you accidentally injure someone or damage their property so that they might have a legal claim against you; and cover for loss or damage to your personal belongings and money. Always check the financial limits on these. For example, an expensive camera might not be covered as most policies have an upper limit per item; it may be best to leave it at home or make sure it's covered on an all risks policy. Other common exclusions include contact lenses and any claims which might arise as a result of being drunk!

Medical expenses are high outside Britain, particularly in the US, so make sure you've enough cover on your holiday insurance to meet these. And check that you're covered for dangerous activities if, for example, you plan to ski, water ski or hire a scooter on a Greek island. Some policies won't cover people over 75 years of age or claims relating to pregnancy.

Take out cover when you book; it doesn't cost any more, and covers you for cancellation immediately. If you have any queries about your holiday insurance check with your travel agent, tour operator, the insurance company your policy is with or the Association of British Insurers, Aldermary House, Queen Street, London EC4, 01-248 4477.

See also: AIR TRAVEL

Holidays

When you book a package holiday the tour operator undertakes to provide you with travel and accommodation as set out in the brochure. If the services listed are not accurate, the company is in breach of contract and you may be able to claim compensation.

So if your dream holiday turns into a real-life hell with half-built hotels, vermin-infested villas or downright rude reps you should complain. If you do this while you're still in the holiday hotspot it gives the company a chance to put things right, and once home you might be entitled to compensation.

While you're still out there tell the rep that you're dissatisfied. Document your grievances – take photographs if possible and keep details of any expenses, such as medical bills. It is even better if you can get other people on the same holiday, at the same hotel or in a neighbouring villa, to back up your claim from their own experience. If the matter isn't resolved, write to the holiday company as soon as you get home, addressing your letter to the consumer relations manager. List all your complaints, giving full details of the holiday. If you don't get a reply send a second letter, once again giving full details and saying how much compensation you're seeking. Don't ask for too much – it has to be in terms of the price of the holiday and the number of faults you found – though in one case a tourist received twice the price as compensation for a disastrous holiday.

Still no success? Keep at them, if you're convinced you have a good case – as far as the managing director if necessary.

If the company offers you a smaller payment than you think is reasonable or money off another holiday you don't want (and who wants to go away again with a company who has let you down?) you might have to resort to court action. Often just the threat of this, a well-worded letter from a solicitor, is enough to push up the size of the cheque; if not, you could take them to the small claims court.

If the tour company is a member of the Association of British Travel

Agents (ABTA), the Association's conciliation service may be able to act as a go-between. But according to a survey carried out by the Consumers' Association, in about half the cases referred to ABTA they don't contact the operator at all because they don't think the holidaymaker has a valid claim. If conciliation fails ABTA also offers an arbitration service as an alternative to taking your case to court (you can't do both).

Some tour operators have tried to duck out of their responsibility through small print at the bottom of their booking forms. For example, by using disclaimers such as 'We shall not be liable for any acts or omissions by persons employed by organisations over which we have no direct control including airlines, hotels and other suppliers of accommodation, and coach operators' or by limiting the amount of compensation which can be paid. Under the Unfair Contract Terms Act such disclaimers or exclusion clauses are only valid if the company can prove that they are reasonable. It is up to the company to do this, so don't be put off claiming by something you've read in the small print.

See also: ABTA, EXCLUSION CLAUSES, SMALL CLAIMS COURT, UNFAIR CONTRACT TERMS ACT

Hospital

If you want to make a complaint while in hospital first mention it to the ward sister who should then report it to the relevant senior person. The hospital administrator is responsible for hospital services while the consultant in charge of your condition is responsible for your medical treatment.

If you've left hospital, or if you prefer this course anyway, write to the administrator of the relevant health authority who will investigate the matter for you. (Ask your Local or Community Health Council – under C or H in phone book – for their address.) In Scotland contact the area Health Board and in Northern Ireland the Central Services Agency.

If you're still not satisfied, you can write to one of the Health Service Commissioners, or Ombudsmen. Although he cannot deal with questions of medical treatment, only with administration, he will be able to tell you whether he can look into your case. The Local or Community Health Council has a leaflet explaining his work. See: HEALTH SERVICE for addresses.

None of the above complaints procedures will help you claim compensation for any distress, injury or suffering you may have experienced as a result of medical treatment. For financial compensation you will

have to go to court, which can be an expensive and lengthy process. If you think you have been the victim of a medical accident contact Action for the Victims of Medical Accidents (AVMA), 24 Southwark Street, London SE1 1TY, 01-403 4744, who can give you help and advice and put you in touch with a solicitor who specialises in such cases. But' remember, in suing a doctor you are embarking upon a long and difficult path.

See also: COMMUNITY HEALTH COUNCIL, DENTISTS, DOCTORS, HEALTH SERVICE

Hotels

If you turn up at a hotel at a reasonable hour they are bound to offer you a room, if they have one, so long as you aren't drunk or either badly dressed or badly behaved. This doesn't apply to guest houses or bed and breakfast establishments.

A hotel can demand a non-returnable deposit and if you cancel, they can keep it; if they can't let the room, they can ask for some of their lost profit too. On the other hand, if you've booked only to turn up and find the hotel is full, with someone else in your room, you can demand compensation for your travelling expenses and any extra costs incurred because of their breach of contract, or the additional cost of a room elsewhere, maybe in a better hotel if that's all that's available.

A hotel must display its charges for both single and double rooms at the door or reception and they must include VAT.

While you are staying in a hotel the proprietor is responsible for any loss or damage to your belongings unless you yourself were to blame. (This doesn't include your car.) He can limit his liability to £50 per item if he displays a notice to this effect in or near reception, but the limit doesn't apply to goods damaged or lost through the hotel's fault. If there's a notice in your room saying the hotel will not accept responsibility for goods not left in the hotel safe, ignore it. If the hotel wants to limit its liability in this way, you must be told when you check in at the latest.

If you have a complaint about the hotel, address it to the manager. If the matter cannot be resolved you could deduct a reasonable amount from the bill and leave your name and address – if the hotel wants more it will sue. Alternatively you could pay the bill but write 'paid under protest' across it; then, when you get home, write to the proprietor or head office and complain.

If the hotel is a member of the British Hotels, Restaurants and Caterers Association, 40 Duke Street, London W1M 6HR, 01-499 6641 they will investigate for you. Failing that and if the matter can't be resolved, you would have to consider whether it's worth taking the hotel to court.

Finding a good hotel, or at least one that suits your needs, is a hit and miss affair at the best of times. If you can't go by personal recommendation then flick through a few hotel guides (remember that with some of them you pay to be included, so a mention isn't necessarily an indication of quality), send for brochures and compare facilities and prices. Our hotel industry has agreed a voluntary Code of Booking Practice with the Department of Trade which covers all hotels, guest houses and bed and breakfast establishments with more than three bedrooms. The Code's aim is to ensure that you know before you book what your stay is likely to cost. You should be given in writing the total charge for the room, including VAT and any obligatory service charge, plus whether the price includes private bathroom facilities or meals and if there is an extra charge to use any of the hotel's advertised facilities such as a sauna or gym.

Housing

For general information about housing in your area contact the housing department of your local council.

For information on housing benefits contact your local DHSS office or dial Freefone DHSS on 0800 666 555. They have a number of leaflets available on all benefits plus a free advisory telephone service.

For disputes over tenancies go to your local Citizens Advice Bureau; they will be able to advise you or if necessary put you in touch with some cheap legal advice.

Shelter, 88 Old Street, London EC1V 9HU, 01-253 0202, is a charity which specialises in helping the homeless.

Information on housing associations or shared ownership schemes is available from The Housing Corporation, 149 Tottenham Court Road, London W1P 0BN.

See also: LODGERS

I

Illegitimacy

Changes in society over the last few decades have brought about changes in our laws on legitimacy. Today, an illegitimate child – one who is born to parents who are not married – has much the same rights as a legitimate one. Usually a birth is registered in the father's name but for illegitimate children this can only be done with the agreement of both parents or if the mother wishes it and has a statutory declaration by a man admitting he is the father; otherwise the child is registered in the mother's name. The father of an illegitimate child cannot demand that the child be registered in his name against the mother's wishes.

The mother of an illegitimate child has sole parental rights and duties, even if the father is paying maintenance, and the only way to ensure a father has access to the child, if the mother doesn't agree, is through the courts.

When it comes to inheritance an illegitimate child is classed as a 'child of the family' if the mother or father die intestate (without making a will), but this is not the case when inheriting from other relatives. If however a will refers to 'children of the family' it is usually taken to include illegitimate children unless stated otherwise.

If a child's parents marry at any time after the baby's birth he or she becomes legitimate from the date of the marriage.

Income Tax

Our tax system is complicated and confusing to say the least and many of us have sneaking fears that we're paying more than we need. So what are our rights and duties? First of all, tax avoidance is quite legal.

Avoidance is where you reduce your tax bill as much as possible by legal means. Tax evasion is illegal.

The onus is on you to tell the taxman of any new income within 12 months of the end of the financial year in which you receive it. The tax year runs from 6 April to 5 April. If you owe tax from previous years, in theory you could be charged interest on the outstanding amount. Any changes in your income should be notified on a tax return. The forms are usually sent to people with complicated financial affairs each year but most of us only get one every few years. If you want a tax return form, ring your local tax office (under Inland Revenue in the phone book) and ask for one.

A single person is responsible for his or her own income tax, while a married man is still responsible for his wife's tax bill although major changes are planned from April 1990. Either partner can ask for a separate assessment in order to keep their income secret. This is not the same as separate taxation and will not affect the total amount paid. Besides your pay other monies subject to income tax include rents received, interest on investments, pensions and some social security benefits.

Most people pay income tax through PAYE (pay as you earn). Your employer deducts the tax from your pay, at source. The Inland Revenue (which administers taxes in Britain) assesses your tax situation and gives your employer the code number which tells him how much to deduct. You will also be sent a notice of your coding. If you change jobs it's vital to take with you a P45 form. Without it your new employer will put you on emergency tax coding which will mean paying over the odds and having to claim back later.

If you have a query about income tax contact your local tax office (under I for Inland Revenue in the phone book) or write to the Inland Revenue, Somerset House, Strand, London WC2.

See also: TAX

Industrial Tribunal

Maternity rights, equal pay, redundancy payments, trade union membership, unfair dismissal – these are among the matters dealt with by industrial tribunals. They are more informal, and so less intimidating, than an ordinary court, and cases are heard by a chairman (a solicitor or barrister) and two lay members, one drawn from a panel of employees' representatives, the other from a panel of employers' representatives.

Leaflets on the working of an industrial tribunal and application forms for hearings are available from your local Employment Office, Job Centre and Citizens Advice Bureau. In all cases a conciliation officer from ACAS (see ACAS) will step in to see if the dispute (between you and your employer) can be settled without a hearing. If not, you can be represented by whom you like – a lawyer, a trade union official, an eloquent friend or spouse – or you can conduct the case yourself. The decision is binding on both parties and appeals can only be made on points of law, for example if you can show that the proper procedures were not gone through. The tribunal has wide powers, for example it can reinstate your job, increase your pay or award compensation. Even if you lose you may be entitled to your travelling expenses and those of witnesses (not legal expenses) and it is very rare that costs are awarded against the applicant – unless the tribunal deems your case to be 'frivolous'.

The Central Office of Industrial Tribunals, 93 Ebury Bridge Road, London SW1W 8RE will give you further information, or ask advice from your trade union, CAB or local law centre.

Inertia Selling

If you've been sent something you didn't order, for example the first book in a set of encyclopaedias, you have probably been the victim of inertia selling. This modern marketing technique lands you with the goods in the hope that you'll find it easier to pay up than send them back.

For the consumer it's irritating and time-consuming, for the trader it's much easier than trying to convince you his product is worth buying. Inertia selling is legal. But, by doing nothing, that's the inertia, you are not incurring any liability. If it happens to you and you don't want the goods, contact the sender immediately, make it clear you don't want whatever it is you've been sent then offer to send them back with a bill for the postage or tell him to come and get them. If you've done this and he doesn't come within 30 days, legally you can keep the goods or dispose of them however you want. Even if you do nothing, the goods are yours after a period of six months.

See: UNSOLICITED GOODS

Information

Your overdraft, your work record, your medical history, your child's progress at school – these are just some examples of personal information about us which is kept on file. Just think of the hundreds of forms we fill in giving information that ideally we wouldn't want everyone to see. Each time we apply for a bank loan, fill in a tax return, claim unemployment benefit, apply for planning permission or buy something on credit we give away a lot about ourselves. Add on that parking fine from a couple of years ago and the insurance policy which matures when you're 60 – it's all kept on file and, as the law stands at the moment, you don't necessarily have the right to see what it says, never mind correct anything that's wrong.

The Data Protection Act, which came into force in 1987, gives us the right to see a copy of any information about ourselves that's held on a computer in return for a small fee. But, the Act only applies to computerised data, so any written or manual records are not covered, and even then certain files can be exempt. For example, doctors can withhold information on medical files where it is likely to cause serious harm to the physical or mental health of the patient. If you want to find out more about the Data Protection Act, ask your local Citizens Advice Bureau for a leaflet issued by the Data Protection Registrar which explains how to go about finding what's held about you. The leaflet has an example of the sort of letter you should write to the company holding the information on computer.

More legislation is in the pipeline; it could include access to all medical files, records held by local authority housing and social work departments and access to school reports.

See also: CREDIT REFERENCE

Injury

If you or your property are injured through the negligence or carelessness of another, you might be able to claim from them. In order to claim successfully in the court you must show: that the person who did the wrong owed you a duty to be careful – for example, the manufacturer of goods owes a duty of care to the person who bought them and to anyone else injured by them; that he or she was negligent; and that injury or economic loss was a result of this carelessness. The law of negligence is complicated and so it is advisable to seek legal advice before embarking on action.

See also: COMPENSATION, CRIMINAL INJURIES COMPENSATION BOARD, HOSPITALS

Instalments

Paying bills by instalments, usually monthly, is a good way to regularise your spending patterns by spreading the financial load and making household budgeting easier. Most large, regular bills can be paid this way including:

RATES: Can be spread over 10 months. Ask your local authority for details.

GAS AND ELECTRICITY BILLS: There are a number of ways to pay including monthly – based on an assessment of your annual consumption divided by 12 – or by buying savings stamps from local showrooms and paying the bill with these when it arrives. Both utilities subscribe to a code of practice which covers the payment of domestic gas and electricity bills; details are available at your local showroom.

TELEPHONE BILLS: Can be paid through a monthly scheme via your bank based on the previous year's bills.

TV LICENCE: You can buy savings stamps at all post offices to help pay for your licence.

INSURANCE: Can often be paid in instalments, particularly car insurance, though sometimes there is a small handling charge.

BUDGET ACCOUNTS: The major banks all offer these to help customers spread the cost of household bills. You estimate all the bills you want to include in the scheme during the year, add them up, divide by 12 and pay that amount into the special account each month. You then pay the bills from that account. Banks usually charge for this service.

Insurance

At some time or other we all need insurance to cover ourselves against financial loss – be it for a holiday, our home and possessions, our car or our lives. Knowing what insurance cover you need is very important and a reputable insurance broker, preferably registered with the Insurance Brokers' Registration Council, 15 St Helen's Place, London

EC3A 6DS, 01-588 4387 should be able to give you any advice you need about the right cover for you. Insurance brokers give independent advice and are not linked with any one insurance company. The Council will also deal with complaints against member brokers.

If you're not happy with the way your insurance company, including their head office, has dealt with your problem, you might be able to get help from the consumer information department of the Association of British Insurers (ABI), Aldermary House, Queen Street, London EC4, 01-248 4477. If the company is a member of the Association they will investigate a complaint. While they will intervene on your behalf with senior management of the company, they can't negotiate a claim for compensation or enforce a decision. Most insurance companies belong to the ABI and abide by their code, which covers insurance practices with the aim of protecting consumers.

Finally, the Insurance Ombudsman Bureau, 31 Southampton Row, London WC1B 5HJ, 01-242 8613 may be able to help sort out a dispute with an insurance company. Provided the company is a member of the scheme, the Ombudsman will look into the complaint and can recommend awards of compensation up to £100,000. He can look into disputes over the way your claim was treated including delays in settlement, but not into a company's poor investment performance, surrender values or bonuses. The company is bound by the decision of the Ombudsman but you can still go to court if you wish.

See also: HOLIDAY INSURANCE, LIFE INSURANCE

Interest Rates

Interest is the extra you pay for the facility of borrowing money or the extra paid to you for lending or investing money. If you're borrowing money, the rate of interest will be reflected in the annual percentage rate (APR), which has to be given by law. If you're investing money, shop around to find out who will pay you the most interest, but bear in mind that for higher interest you may have to leave your cash invested for longer periods.

See also: CREDIT (for APR)

Irradiation

Around the world irradiation is being used, on spices in America, wheat in Canada, garlic in Italy, to preserve food. The food is passed through the waves given off by radioactive material. The waves penetrate the food, leaving behind a trail of ionised particles of water. These produce chemicals which kill many of the organisms that cause decay, growth cells that make some vegetables sprout and tiny pests that accumulate in crops of spices or cereals. The food then stays fresher for longer but not indefinitely; for this such high doses would be necessary they would destroy the taste and would be higher than the levels approved by the World Health Organisation (WHO).

The WHO has passed irradiation but so far individual countries have only approved its use for certain foods. In Britain the Government confirmed its ban on its use in February 1988.

On the plus side British food manufacturers say it will cut costs and make foods such as fruit and vegetables, fish and meat cheaper for the consumer. Their greater keeping qualities will give us a wider choice of foods all the year round and, they say, our foods will actually be healthier because fewer or no chemicals need be added to preserve them.

J

Junk Mail

Plop! Another brochure lands on the doormat – this time you've been promised inclusion in the biggest prize draw ever or yet another credit company wants to put their card in your wallet. 'Junk' or unsolicited mail, to give it its posh name, is growing at such a huge rate that the postal service need never fear extinction. But just how do those companies get our names and what can you do to clear the clutter off the mat?

The answer to the first is simple. Although you may not subscribe to any mail order companies, book clubs or the like, you probably have a telephone and like to vote. The local phone directory and the electoral roll are two easy sources of names and addresses. Then there's the time you were asked to write your address on the back of that cheque in a shop. Your work may give you away, too, through lists of members of your professional, club or trade association. Apply to the council for planning permission and the local double glazing firm can soon catch on to you from your address printed in the local paper. And if you've just bought shares, watch out as lists of shareholders are held at Companies House and anyone can look you up there.

If you still think you're safe, take heed. Companies can buy or rent names and addresses. There are list brokers who actually specialise in compiling lists and selling them.

To try to stop the steady stream of unwanted mail you could send the offending literature back in a plain unstamped envelope; the company will then have to pay a surcharge on unpaid post as well as the cost of the missing stamps. Or when you order goods by post, make it a condition of sale (write it on the order form) that the company doesn't sell or rent your name. Try spelling your name incorrectly and see whether you get any literature from other companies with this same misspelling.

It's worth taking the official line too by writing to the Mailing Preference Service, Freepost 22, London W1E 7EZ. If you fill in their application form they'll have your name deleted from all future lists compiled by their member companies. On the other hand, if you actually *want* to attract extra mail you can ask the service to add your name to the lists!

Jury Service

Anyone between the ages of 18 and 65 on the electoral register is liable to be called for jury service. The following are ineligible: judges, magistrates, lawyers, the police, prison officers, probation officers and clergymen, plus anyone who has been in prison during the last 10 years. Anyone who has been sentenced to five years or more in prison is disqualified for life. The following people can ask to be excused: Members of Parliament, the armed forces and the medical profession. If you are summoned to appear on a jury and it's difficult to serve at that time, for example you are going on holiday, it's worth writing back to the jury summoning officer (address on summoning papers) and explaining the circumstances. Whatever you do, don't ignore the summons or you could be fined.

K

Kitemark

The Kitemark is the British Standards Institution's trademark displayed on goods, samples of which have been independently tested to the appropriate British Standard. It appears on all sorts of things from motorcycle safety helmets to lawn mowers. More than 800 companies participate in the scheme and ensure their products comply. Buying Kitemarked goods is an important way of ensuring the quality of what you buy and the BSI itself will look into any problems relating to goods bearing the symbol. If you want to know more about standards of products carrying the Kitemark contact BSI on (0908) 220908.

See also: BRITISH STANDARDS INSTITUTION

L

Labels

If a label on goods contains information which is untrue, for example if you are told eggs are free range when they're not, you can claim your money back from the shop under the Sale of Goods Act because the goods are not as described. The seller might also be committing the offence of misdescription so you should inform your local trading standards or consumer protection department.

In law some goods have to be labelled in certain ways to give us important information which might affect our choice of what to buy. For example, a label may have to show the goods' country of origin, the manufacturer's or packer's name and address, the weight and contents of a packet or include specific warnings, as with cigarettes.

See also: FOOD LABELLING

Landlords

If you're tempted to let your home, or a room in it, it pays to be wise to a few facts. If you have a mortgage, you should get the lender's permission first. Most mortgage agreements impose this in case the house has to be repossessed or you need to sell it yourself.

A council tenant should ask the council's permission before deciding to take lodgers. It can only refuse on grounds that it would lead to overcrowding. Your rates won't go up if you just let one or two rooms, but if you are really running a guest house you will be assessed at a higher business level. If you turn part of your home into a self-contained flat, this will be rated separately. You must not, of course, do this to a council house, nor may you sub-let.

Spell out from the start what's included in the rent, how phone bills are to be paid and arrangements for laundry, and tell a tenant your views on visitors, noise, smoking and anything else you're concerned about. So long as you live in the house as well you are a 'resident' landlord and anyone sharing with you has no long-term security. Your agreement is legally binding whether or not you put it in writing, so giving a rent book doesn't affect either your position or theirs. If your agreement is weekly or monthly and you want your lodger to leave, you will have to give four weeks' notice in writing. If the tenancy is for a fixed term it simply ends when the time is up.

If the tenant won't leave, ultimately you would have to get a court order to get them out. The court must give you possession if the house or flat concerned is your own home, but it can postpone the moving date for up to three months.

Major changes are in the pipeline, which will affect both landlords' and tenants' rights in the future. For further details of these ask at your local Citizens Advice Bureau or phone the Housing Centre Trust on 01-637 4202.

See also: LODGERS

Laser Scanning

Pioneered in the US in the 1970s, laser scanning, or electronic point of sale (EPOS) to give it its posh name, has revolutionised British supermarket shopping. The system works by linking bar codes – those stripes found on nearly all our groceries as well as many other products – with a central computer. The bar code is scanned by laser and the computer then relays information, such as the price and a description of the goods, back to the till which prints it on the receipt.

Although there were some initial technical difficulties with the system, now largely ironed out, it makes shopping quicker, minimises the chance of checkout error and gives detailed receipts so you can spot a mistake quickly. Stock control is also more efficient. The computer registers each sale so that staff know when to restock shelves and reorder. This looks like being only the first step towards a fully automated checkout. Next to look out for is electronic fund transfer at point of sale (EFTPOS) where your bill is directly debited from your bank account.

Laundries

In the past some unscrupulous launderers and dry cleaners have been notorious for trying to cheat us out of our legal rights by using sneaky exclusion clauses which either limit the amount of compensation they have to pay if they damage a garment or get them out of paying anything at all. But thanks to the Unfair Contract Terms Act this is no longer the case; any such clauses now have to be reasonable to be valid.

If you have a complaint about a launderer or cleaner, go back to the shop, explain what has happened and ask them to put it right. If the matter can't be corrected, for example if the garment is too badly damaged, then you are entitled to compensation. How much will depend on how old the item is, how much wear you've had out of it and how badly damaged it is.

Many launderers and dry cleaners are members of the ABLCRS, the Association of British Laundry, Cleaning and Rental Services Ltd, Lancaster Gate House, 319 Pinner Road, Harrow, Middlesex HA1 4HX, 01-863 7755. Members are bound by a code of practice by which, among other provisions, members agree to pay fair compensation to a customer for loss or damage due to the member's negligence. If a problem isn't resolved between the customer and the member, the Association's customer advisory service can try to conciliate. They could send the garment to a lab to be independently tested (of course you or the launderer could choose to do this anyway). You will probably have to pay but the money will be refunded if your complaint is upheld. The member must abide by any findings of the Association but you can still go to court if you're not happy with the outcome.

See also: DRY CLEANING, UNFAIR CONTRACT TERMS ACT

Law Centres
In some areas neighbourhood law centres offer free legal advice. To find your nearest law centre look under L in the phone book.

Law Society
The Law Society regulates the behaviour of solicitors in England and Wales. Until recently it also dealt with consumer complaints against solicitors but now in England and Wales that work is dealt with by the Solicitors Complaints Bureau. The Law Society is at 113 Chancery Lane, London WC2A 1PL, 01-242 1222. There are separate societies for Scotland and Northern Ireland. The Law Society of Northern Ireland is at Law Society House, 90 Victoria Street, Belfast BT1 3JZ, (0232) 231614 and the Law Society of Scotland at 26–27 Drumsheugh Gardens, Edinburgh EH3 7YR, 031-226 7411.

See also: LAY OBSERVERS, SOLICITORS

Lawyers

The legal profession in Britain is divided into two – solicitors and barristers (called advocates in Scotland). The former deal directly with clients on a wide range of legal problems but can only speak for you in the lower courts while the latter have to be approached through a solicitor and appear in the higher courts.

See also: BARRISTERS, SOLICITORS

Lay Observers

The Lord Chancellor has appointed the Lay Observer (there are separate ones for Scotland and Northern Ireland), who is neither a solicitor nor a barrister, to look at complaints against solicitors. If you have made a complaint and are dissatisfied either with the way the Solicitors Complaints Bureau or the regional Law Society has handled it or with their decision at the end of the investigation, then you can write to the Lay Observer, Royal Courts of Justice, Strand, London WC2A 2LL, 01-936 6695. The Lay Observer can't re-investigate the complaint or give you legal advice. His job is to examine the treatment of your complaint and decide whether it was investigated fully and fairly. You must write to the Lay Observer within three months of being given the decision on your complaint (six months in Scotland). The Lay Observer for Scotland is at 30 Castle Street, Edinburgh EH2 3HT, 031-226 2503. The Lay Observer for Northern Ireland is at Clarendon House, 9–21 Adelaide Street, Belfast BT2 8ND.

See also: SOLICITORS

LEA

See: EDUCATION, SCHOOLS

Legal Aid

Going to court can be a costly business but many people can get help with fees through legal aid in the following ways:

THE GREEN FORM SCHEME: So called because of the colour of the form. You go to a solicitor, give him or her details of your income and savings and he or she fills in the green form, adds up the figures and can tell you whether you qualify for legal advice and assistance. If you do, it covers most everyday legal problems including divorce and maintenance cases, employment rights, landlord and tenant disputes, and making a will. Under this scheme a solicitor can give advice, write letters and prepare a

case for you to go before a tribunal. He cannot represent you in court except in domestic proceedings heard in the Magistrate's Court (not in a divorce as this has to be decided in the County Court).

WHO QUALIFIES? If you're receiving Income Support or Family Credit and have few savings you won't have to pay a penny. If not, then you may have to pay a contribution or may not qualify at all. Your local Citizens Advice Bureau will be able to advise you on how likely you are to qualify and put you in touch with a local solicitor who operates the scheme. Or look out for the legal aid sticker in a solicitor's window.

It is important to remember that all legal aid is more of a loan than a gift in that the cost of it has to be paid back out of anything you recover from the action – unless this would cause great hardship, of course.

CIVIL LEGAL AID: This covers non-criminal court proceedings. It may follow on from the Green Form Scheme or you might qualify for this when you didn't for the other because the financial limits are higher. If you think you might qualify, ask your solicitor. He doesn't work out the figures but he, or she, can tell you whether civil legal aid is available for such cases. Who qualifies is decided by the Department of Health and Social Security, who send you a form to fill in; then the legal aid office decides whether you have reasonable grounds for going to court. Once again the legal aid fund takes its charges out of anything you win.

CRIMINAL LEGAL AID: Under British law anyone charged with a crime is presumed innocent until proven guilty and is entitled to a defence. If you are charged, ask the court straight away for legal aid. If the court decide it's in the interests of justice for you to be legally represented, they can grant legal aid. Most cases heard in the Crown Court are legally aided. There are financial limits and you might be called upon to make a monetary contribution to the cost of your defence.

See also: FIXED FEE INTERVIEW, GREEN FORM SCHEME

Life Insurance

Life insurance salesmen are the butt of many a joke and it's hardly surprising as the job attracts some of the sharpest sellers in the business. Even though salesmen will tell you otherwise (it's all commission to them) some people probably don't need life insurance at all. For example, if you're young, have no real financial commitments and no dependants your money would probably be better spent elsewhere. Life insurance is a must if anyone would suffer financially if you died. If you are interested in life cover, go to an insurance broker who can give you details on a wide variety of schemes, offered by a number of companies. He should be able to advise you on the best one to suit your needs.

All life insurance pays out on death but some – endowment policies – can be paid out on an agreed date, for example on your retirement or in a set number of years. Endowment policies are often sold as a long-term investment but you could get a better return for your money elsewhere. The more money it will pay out eventually the higher the premiums you'll have to pay. Policies for whole life or endowment can be with or without profits; with profits is more expensive but pays a sum on top of the agreed amount.

Since the Financial Services Act not only do insurance brokers have to be registered but the advice they give must be the best in the circumstances. If you have a complaint about an insurance company or broker first complain direct to them. If this fails refer the matter, preferably in writing, to their head office. If the company is a member of the Association of British Insurers (ABI) they can investigate your complaint but they can't negotiate a claim for compensation or enforce a decision. The ABI are at Aldermary House, Queen Street, London EC4, 01-248 4477.

Finally, the Insurance Ombudsman Bureau, 31 Southampton Row, London WC1 5HJ, 01-242 8613, may be able to help. Provided the company is a member of the scheme, the ombudsman will look into the complaint and can recommend awards up to £100,000. If you don't accept his findings you can go to court.

See also: FINANCIAL SERVICES ACT, INSURANCE

Loans

See: BORROWING

Local Authorities

Much of the day-to-day running of our lives is done by the local authority, from public transport to recreational facilities, from housing to highways. In spite of local government reorganisations it can still be confusing as to who is in charge of what. If you're not sure who to contact ask at your local Citizens Advice Bureau (under C in the phone book).

If you have a complaint about council services, first discuss it with the person performing the service. He, or she, may have limited power but if it is something straightforward might be able to sort out the difficulty quickly. If that fails, put your complaint in writing to the chief officer of the relevant department, who could be the Director of Education, Chief Planning Officer and so on. He has a duty to look into the public's complaints. If that too fails it's on to the Town Clerk, sometimes called the Chief Executive Officer.

If you're having little success with the authority itself you should find out the name of your local councillor and tell him or her about your problem. Elected by you, he has a duty to you to look into a complaint about policy or the way it is being interpreted. Finally, in any matter where you think you have been mistreated by the authority's action, or indeed inaction, you can ask the local authority ombudsman to help. There are five ombudsmen covering England, Scotland and Wales. They will look into complaints about local authorities, planning boards, water and police authorities. They can investigate complaints about unjustified delay, discrimination and faulty ways of doing things. They can't, however, question the council's decision. For example, they can't investigate a rise in the rates. The ombudsman can order that you be paid compensation or ask the council to put the matter right, although the findings are not binding on the authority.

You can write direct to the appropriate ombudsman, whose addresses are: Commissioners for Local Administration for Greater London, South East, South West, West Midlands and East Anglia, 21 Queen Anne's Gate, London SW1H 9BU, 01-222 5622; ... for North and East Midlands, 29 Castlegate, York, YO1 1RN; ... for Scotland, Princess House, 5 Shandwick Place, Edinburgh EH2 4RG; ... for Wales, Derwen House, Court Road, Bridgend, Mid-Glamorgan CF31 1BN; and ... for Northern Ireland, Progressive House, 33 Wellington Place, Belfast, BT1 6HM.

See also: TRADING STANDARDS, and, for individual departments, see

COUNCIL HOMES, EDUCATION, ENVIRONMENTAL HEALTH, PLANNING PERMISSION, POLICE, WATER

Lodgers

When viewing a prospective new home make sure you ask the right questions. Draw up a list before you go that includes asking about what the rent covers and any particular requirements you may have, for example, if you're a smoker, practise drums at night or need somewhere to store a bicycle. Ask for a rent book; although this is not necessary legally it could avoid disputes as you always know how much you've paid. Agree when the rent should be paid. Whether it's weekly or monthly makes no difference to your rights as a tenant, but one may be more convenient to you than the other. If you are asked for a deposit, make sure you get a receipt that states clearly whether it is against rent or possible damage. And keep a note of the value of any breakages when they happen.

Legally, under the Housing Act 1980, your tenancy with a resident landlord is counted as a 'restricted contract' so that when the period is up or your landlady gives you notice you will have to go. But if you feel undue pressure is being applied to get you out – i.e. you're harassed – the law is on your side. Seek help from the housing department of your local council or the nearest Citizens Advice Bureau (under C in the phone book).

Finding lodgings is often best done by word of mouth. But also read the small ads in the local paper or cards in newsagents' windows. Students can often find digs through college accommodation services and many landladies prefer students who leave the house for the summer.

If you want to know more the Department of the Environment produces a series of leaflets on tenants' and landlords' rights. Copies are available from your local authority, law centre or Citizens Advice Bureau.

See also: LANDLORDS

Lotteries

A lottery is a scheme by which prizes are given by lot or chance and where no skill is involved. Under the Lotteries and Amusements Act 1976 a lottery is illegal unless it is promoted by a registered society to make money for their own purposes, or is private, which would include those organised by local authorities.

See also: COMPETITIONS

M

Mail Order

We spend more than £3,000 million a year on shopping by post. It saves us time, shoe leather and petrol. But, for all its convenience, mail order comes top of the consumer problem list among *Woman* readers. To be fair to the mail order companies, some of the hassles we bring on ourselves. The *Woman* mail order offers department gets hundreds of orders every year with no address to send the goods to. So, whether you're buying from a catalogue or answering an advert in a newspaper or magazine, here's a checklist to follow before you post your order:

- Read the small print. Some companies will automatically send you another colour or style when they're out of stock, rather than refund you. Go for companies which offer money back guarantees or goods 'on approval'.
- Write your order clearly – preferably in capital letters to avoid any misreading by the company.
- If you have to send money, don't send cash. Use cheques or postal orders so that you have a record of what you've paid.
- Set a time limit. To give yourself extra protection against delay write on the order form that if the goods don't come within a certain period of time you will want your money back. Usually the offer will indicate how long you should allow for delivery.
- Keep the company's full name and address plus details of your order. Also keep details of the magazine or newspaper when you are ordering through an advertisement. Always keep copies of any letters you send.

If you lose the company's address, the following might be able to help you: directory enquiries if you can remember the name and roughly where they're based; the local consumer protection or trading standards office; the Mail Order Traders' Association (MOTA), 25 Castle Street, Liverpool L2 4TD, 051-236 7581 – many companies which sell through catalogues are members and they will try to find addresses; if the ad was in a newspaper or magazine, ask the advertising manager of the publication concerned to give you the company's address.

Some of the more common problems with mail order companies include goods not arriving, goods arriving damaged or faulty and computer errors which are slow to alter your account or fail to acknowledge returned goods. If goods don't arrive, ring the customer relations manager of the company (if a large order is involved it may be better to put it in writing), quoting any reference number you have, the date of your order, catalogue numbers and prices. If you want a refund say so now; otherwise give them a further 10 days (or whatever you think is reasonable in the circumstances) to deliver but say that after that date you will require a refund. Send any letter by recorded delivery so you can be sure they receive it. Goods that are damaged or faulty when you get them should be sent straight back (although if they were in good order when they started the journey and have been damaged by the carrier, strictly damage in transit cannot be blamed on the seller). Send a covering letter (keep a copy) explaining why they've been returned and get a certificate of posting when sending them back. Your rights when you buy by mail order are the same as when buying from a shop and you can demand a refund for faulty goods under the Sale of Goods Act. You're also entitled to ask for the cost of postage.

Computer errors are usually really human errors. If your letters, returned goods and so on have had no effect, it's probably best to phone the company to check you're not a computer error victim.

Unfortunately it isn't unknown for mail order companies, particularly small ones, to go out of business. If you find out early enough write to the Receiver to register yourself on the list of creditors; the local consumer protection or trading standards office will be able to tell you his name and address. But often in circumstances like this, after paying what's owed the taxman, staff and VAT, there may be little money left for customers.

When buying from a catalogue choose one which is a member of MOTA or, if buying books or records, choose a member of the Association of Mail Order Publishers (AMOP), 1 New Burlington Street, London W1X 1FD; both operate a code of practice which gives benefits in addition to your legal rights. If you're buying from a newspaper or magazine advert, check the publication is covered by a mail order protection scheme which ensures that you don't suffer if the trader goes bust. Write to the advertising manager of the publication and don't delay or you could lose out. If you pay by credit card, and the trader goes bust, you may have a claim against the credit company for your money so long as the goods cost £100 or more.

See also: CATALOGUES, INERTIA SELLING

Maintenance

In Britain it is usually considered that a husband has a duty to maintain his wife and children and, in the event of the marriage splitting up, to continue to make maintenance payments in respect of the children and sometimes the wife. If the wife was the main breadwinner she could be expected to pay maintenance.

In recent years there has been a change of emphasis in matrimonial law, when it comes to financial settlements, to what is called the 'clean break' principle. Courts are now encouraged, wherever possible, to arrange one-off financial settlements or to order maintenance payments for limited periods instead of granting meal tickets for life.

In assessing maintenance the court will take into account factors such as the length of the marriage, children (maintenance is payable until they are 18), the age of the parties, whether you work or have a chance of finding a job and your spouse's income. How much is paid and for how long will depend on individual circumstances.

A common law husband has no duty to maintain his 'wife' but must maintain his children.

While the divorce is going through it is usual for the husband (or wife if she is the main breadwinner) to continue to keep the family. If they don't the other party can apply to the court for an interim maintenance order or, as a final resort, ask the local DHSS about entitlement to state benefits.

So long as maintenance payments have not been dismissed by the court either party can go back and ask for them to be varied at a later date if the circumstances of either have changed in some material way, for example your former spouse's income is greatly increased.

See also: DIVORCE

Maintenance Contracts

Maintenance contracts are contracts of service taken out on goods we buy, the most common being on washing machines or other 'white' goods. They tend to be expensive but usually cover you against most failures, including those due to wear and tear. Both parts and labour are usually covered and some include an annual service. You can generally call in the service engineer as often as you like without charge. While they do give some peace of mind, and protect you against unexpected big bills, a Consumers' Association *Which?* magazine survey showed that they represent poor value and that in most cases you'd be better off paying for repairs as you go along. For example, they worked out that a five-year maintenance contract on a dishwasher would add up to four times the estimated cost of repairs over the same period. Of course, if you were unlucky enough to buy a rogue machine you might be grateful for such a deal.

But remember that the shop should supply you with goods of merchantable quality and will be liable under the Sale of Goods Act if the goods are not reasonably durable, whether you have a maintenance contract or not.

Marriage

For a marriage to be valid it must conform with the Marriage Act 1949. A marriage in Britain must take place either in the Church of England (or Wales), where the reading of banns is usually required, or in a church of another denomination or a register office, when a certificate must be obtained from the Superintendent Registrar. If you're not getting married in a Church of England ceremony you need to get the certificate from the register office first. There are two types of certificate: one without a licence which allows you 21 days in which to get married after giving notice of your intention; and one with a licence which means you only have to give two days' notice (one clear day between giving notice and getting married). Once you've got your certificate you can marry in the local register office or in any church or designated religious building.

You can marry, in Britain, at 16 with parental consent. If the parents are divorced, the parent who has custody must consent. At 18 you can marry without consent. The law does not recognise homosexual marriage.

There are certain people, mostly close relatives, whom you can't marry. For a woman they include your father, son, grandfather, grandson, brother, uncle and nephew. Also included are your mother's husband, grandmother's husband, husband's son, husband's grandson (unless both are over 21 and the younger wasn't at any time before the age of 18 a child of the family in relation to the older), husband's father (unless both are over 21 and both husband and husband's mother are dead), daughter's husband (unless both are over 21 and both daughter and father of daughter are dead). For a man they include your mother and so on.

A woman is under no legal obligation to change her surname on marriage, but a child of the marriage is usually registered under the father's name.

See also: ILLEGITIMACY, MAINTENANCE

Medicines

The sale of medicines is strictly controlled. General sales list medicines can be bought over the counter in a pharmacy for everyday illnesses. Some, like aspirin and paracetamol, can only be sold in small packets if there's no pharmacist present but, for example, in a supermarket there is no control over the number of small packets you can buy. However, there is control over how they are packed – in sealed dosage units, foil or blister packs, or in a child-proof container. Some medicines can only be bought when a pharmacist is present and even though he, or she, may not make the sale, he has to be aware it is going on. The pharmacist has the right to refuse a sale if he suspects addiction to a particular medicine or feels it is in the patient's own interests to withhold it. Finally, some medicines are available only on a doctor's prescription. Medicines now have to be labelled by the pharmacist showing how they should be used and stored.

See also: CHEMISTS

Merchantable Quality

A skirt with a broken zip, a shirt with a frayed seam and a shoe with a heel which drops off have one thing in common. They are not of merchantable quality, and under the Sale of Goods Act you are entitled to your money back from the shop where you bought them. This quaint old legal term forms the very basis of our shoppers' rights. To be of merchantable quality goods should be reasonably fit for their normal purpose and what is reasonable will depend to some extent on the price paid and how they were described to you.

See also: SALE OF GOODS ACT

MIRAS
See: MORTGAGES

Misleading Prices
Under the Trade Descriptions Act 1968 and the Bargain Offers Order (these price provisions will be replaced soon by the Consumer Protection Act 1987) it is against the law to give consumers a misleading price indication about any goods, services, accommodation or facilities. Examples of some of the claims not allowed include 'worth £20 – our price £10' and comparisons with a previous price offered by the trader unless he has had them on sale at that price at that shop or another branch for at least 28 consecutive days in the last six months (although he can wriggle out of this by putting up a sign saying this condition has not been met). With certain goods it is also illegal to compare a shop's price with that recommended by a manufacturer; these include electrical domestic appliances, electronic goods, carpets and furniture. Some price comparisons are allowed and these include introductory offers (if the time they last is specified), comparisons with a competitor if they name the competitor and different prices for different categories of customer such as pensioners or cash buyers.
See also: BARGAINS

Mock Auctions
If you've ever been attracted by the fast-talking sales patter of a street seller auctioning his wares you've probably been ensnared in a mock auction. Often found at the seaside, these sales are dubbed 'mock' auctions because they don't sell to the highest bidder. The clever salesman develops a fever pitch of excitement in onlookers in order to sell his goods, often substandard, be they towels, transistors or teddy bears. The Mock Auctions Act 1961 is an attempt to outlaw these sales. It defines a mock auction as one where goods are sold at a price lower than the highest bid or where the right to bid is restricted to those customers who have either already bought something or agreed to buy (often they don't know at that point what they've agreed to buy) or where goods are given away as an inducement to buy. The Act doesn't apply in Northern Ireland.

Mortgages
Gone are the days when you had to grovel for a mortgage; today there seems to be an endless stream of people wanting to lend us money to buy

a home of our own. But how do you choose the best deal to suit you? Don't be swayed by too generous offers of loans which will eat up the greater part of your earnings. Two and a half times your income plus your partner's is usually a safe guide and it is still the most common sum done by building societies and banks.

There aren't many properties that would-be lenders regard as unsuitable but it's worth knowing about the few categories on which they might refuse to lend. Short life properties – they'll want to be sure the property has an expected life of at least 30 years otherwise there could be problems selling later on. Similarly, leasehold properties where the lease doesn't have long to run. Flats converted from a house used to be more of a problem than they are now but the lender might want to be satisfied as to the quality of the conversion. Freehold flats sometimes get a straight 'no' from lenders because of legal problems over maintenance.

Before you decide on whether to borrow from a building society, a bank or one of the new lenders such as the Mortgage Corporation, compare interest rates. Some offer special deals such as lower interest rates for first-time buyers or help with other costs associated with house buying. Your bank might be keen to lend, because they know your financial situation better than most, but you may prefer to keep your property business separate from your other money. Building societies have the track record and are committed to property buying.

Basically loans to buy property fall into two main types – repayment and endowment. The one thing to remember when you start loan hunting is that there are plenty of people with an interest in fixing an endowment loan for you – they can earn a fat commission from a life insurance company on the policy that accompanies the endowment mortgage.

REPAYMENT METHOD: Still the most common type of mortgage. Each month you pay back a little bit of the capital you have borrowed plus interest on the outstanding loan. Unless interest rates change you pay exactly the same amount each month and as the years go by the proportion of interest decreases as the outstanding loan goes down. Most people who take out a repayment mortgage also arrange for a mortgage protection policy. This is a cheap form of life insurance that means the loan will be paid off automatically if you should die. Whoever grants you the mortgage will advise you on this.

A low-start repayment mortgage is a variation on the ordinary repayment mortgage. You get maximum tax relief in the early years of the mortgage and therefore pay less at the start. In the long run you can end up paying more with this system.

ENDOWMENT METHOD: With this type of mortgage you pay back none of the capital during the time of the loan. Instead you pay interest on the full amount of the loan every month, plus a premium to an insurance company for an endowment policy. At the end of the mortgage period the proceeds of the endowment policy are used to pay off the mortgage. In its favour you have built-in life cover if anything happens to you before the loan is paid off.

There are three main types of endowment mortgage: with-profits, without-profits and low-cost endowments. On with-profits, you pay a higher premium for your insurance each month, but bonuses are added to the policy's value so that at the end of the term you can repay the mortgage and collect a substantial lump sum. This is the most expensive form of mortgage, but could suit people who have the money to put aside and would like to be forced to do some long-term saving. On a without-profits policy, the proceeds at the end are just enough to pay off the mortgage loan. Low-cost endowment is where you pay a lower premium than on a with-profits policy, but the assumption is that by the end of the mortgage term the proceeds of your insurance (with bonuses added in) will be enough to repay the loan with an additional lump sum for you. Endowment mortgages used to have tax advantages, but no longer, and in recent years they have sometimes carried lower interest rates than repayment loans to attract borrowers.

PENSION MORTGAGES are relatively new. They allow self-employed people and employees who are not in a company pension scheme to use a pension plan instead of a life assurance policy to pay off their mortgage. It works in a similar way to an endowment with the advantage of tax relief on the pension plan payments.

Check when you take out any mortgage what the lender's attitude would be if you moved before the term had ended. Some have financial penalties for paying off the home loan early. Also check whether an endowment mortgage can be transferred to another property, and remember that if you want to cash it in before the term the surrender value might be low in the early years. Some lenders also charge a higher interest rate for loans over a certain amount so shop around if you want a large loan.

One ray of light – the Chancellor still allows us tax relief on the interest we pay on our mortgage loan. We get relief on a loan up to £30,000 per property. The tax relief is adjusted through MIRAS, Mortgage Interest Relief at Source.

Motor Agents Association
See: CARS

Moving House
Moving house is a major upheaval in anyone's life and who to trust with your worldly goods is quite a headache. More than half a million of us move each year and 60 per cent call in professional removal firms to help. When Actionwoman put removal firms to the test we found that you can pay up to twice as much for the same job, so our advice is to shop around. When questioned, most of the firms were vague about the packing materials they used, how many men were being paid for and about insurance cover – though all offered some form of insurance.

Goods insurance cover is vital, while your possessions are on the move and also if they go into storage. Check with your insurance company to see if your household contents policy already covers you for moving or whether it can be extended by paying an additional premium. If they will cover you, compare this with the removal firm's insurance cover.

According to the Office of Fair Trading there are still plenty of cowboys in the removal business and common complaints include late arrival, stopping off at the pub *en route*, damage to furniture, goods lost in store, broken china, bills for double the amount of the estimate or being caught out by small print in a contract limiting the firm's liability.

When choosing a firm, if possible go on a personal recommendation from a satisfied customer. Get more than one written quotation. Check whether it is a quotation or an estimate – the latter is not binding as to price – and don't accept a firm's offer to find other quotes for you – they could be going to one of their subsidiaries. Pay a rate for the job rather than by the hour. Some firms offer the hourly alternative but you can be caught out if the packing and loading takes longer than you expected – and you will pay dearly for that reviving cuppa you offer the men. Always get a quote and get the firm's estimator to come and look in person at what the job entails. Some firms, particularly if you employ one from the area you are moving to, send you forms to fill in and base their estimate on this, but this makes a proper assessment of the job very difficult.

Ask about the packing materials they will use. For example, will they use white paper for china or will you be left with a newspaper imprint on your dinner service? Discuss any special packing, for example whether a separate crate will be needed for art treasures or lifting gear for a grand piano. If they want you to pack your own goods, or you choose to pack for yourself, beware, your insurance cover could be affected.

Look for a firm which is a member of the British Association of Removers, 277 Gray's Inn Road, London WC1X 8SY. All their members are vetted for standards of service.

N

National Consumer Council

An independent pressure group which, though funded by government, voices the concerns and causes of consumers in general to the Government and other interested bodies. Among other things the Council lobbies for changes in legislation to protect consumers, where necessary, and carries out and compiles reports. They can't advise or intervene in individual cases. Their address is 20 Grosvenor Gardens, London SW1W 0DH. The Scottish Consumer Council is at 314 St Vincent Street, Glasgow G3 8XW, The Welsh Consumer Council at Castle Buildings, Womanby Street, Cardiff CF1 2BN, and in Northern Ireland, the General Consumer Council (which will also deal directly with consumer complaints about electricity and public utilities) is at Elizabeth House, 116 Hollywood Road, Belfast BT4 1MY.

National Federation of Consumer Groups

The Federation is the central organisation for voluntary local consumer groups. You can join as an individual member or the Federation can put you in touch with a group in your area or help you start one up. Groups keep an eye on local goods and services, draw up reports and campaign, where necessary, for improvements. For further information send an s.a.e. to Mrs D. Freeman, Flat 1, 31 Sussex Square, Brighton BN2 5AB, (0273) 602816.

National House Building Council

If you're buying a new house or one that is under 10 years old make sure that the builder is on the register of the National House Building Council. If the property has an NHBC certificate this shows it has been built to a certain standard and the Council will make sure certain defects which could occur during the first 10 years of the property's life are put right. The guarantee remains with the property and so can be passed on to benefit future occupants. Although it is a welcome safeguard when buying a property, beware, not all structural defects are covered by the certificate.

If you want general information write to the NHBC at 58 Portland Place, London W1; for information on registering or claims, write to them at Chiltern Avenue, Amersham, Buckinghamshire HP6 5AP.

National Insurance

All employees and self-employed people pay national insurance contributions to qualify for certain state benefits including a pension and unemployment benefit. The amount you pay depends on your earnings, and the level of benefit you receive on the contributions paid. In the past married women could opt to pay a reduced national insurance contribution but missed out on many benefits.

For further details on national insurance contributions and the many benefits available contact your local Department of Health and Social Security office, under H in the phone book, or call Freefone 0800 666 555.

See also: BENEFITS, ONE-PARENT FAMILIES, REDUNDANCY

National Savings

National Savings (NS) products are sold by the Government to raise money to make up the difference between government spending and income raised from other sources, such as tax. They include: National Savings Certificates, some of which are index-linked, others which pay a fixed amount after five years; and a Yearly Plan which is a regular monthly investment scheme, the money from which is then used to buy certificates. Apart from the novel idea of investing in the Government, the major advantage of NS Certificates is that the return is tax free.

Other NS products, all available over the counter at the Post Office, include an Ordinary Account, similar to a bank deposit account, an Investment Account on which the interest is higher but where you have to give one month's notice of a withdrawal, and Deposit and Income bonds, both of which pay a good rate of interest while the latter can be used to give you a monthly income. National Savings are better viewed as longer term investments and full details of all the schemes are available in leaflets from the Post Office.

See also: PREMIUM BONDS

Negligence

The legal term for carelessness. If through someone's carelessness you or your property is damaged, you may be able to sue for compensation on grounds of that person's negligence. That person would have to owe you a duty of care, be it the local authority to maintain the pavement or your neighbour to keep his boa constrictor under control, and you would have to prove that what happened was his fault. This can be a major problem, but there are signs that the law is changing, at least in some cases. If you suffer injury or damage to your property because of a defective product, under the Consumer Protection Act 1987 you can now in some cases claim compensation from the manufacturer without having to prove it was his fault (so-called strict liability). It is always advisable to seek legal advice before pursuing any action for negligence.

Neighbourhood Watch

A community-based movement to help protect your property and keep crime down. If your neighbourhood has a watch scheme it might help reduce the premiums on your house contents insurance policy. If you're interested in starting up a scheme in your area contact your local crime prevention officer, through the police, who should be only too happy to talk to your group and advise on how to run the scheme most effectively.

Neighbours

Neighbours are a fact of suburban life, and no matter how well you get on with them there are going to be times when you wish they lived next door to someone else. The police are usually unwilling to intervene in disputes with 'them next door' and frankly it is always better in the long run to try to sort out a problem peacefully between yourselves. But what can you do if your powers of persuasion fail?

· NOISY PARTY: In some areas the police will respond to calls to ask for the music to be turned down, but noise has to be continuous or repeated for legal action to be taken, such as an injunction to stop them playing the drums at 3 am! If you're in doubt ask the local environmental health department for advice, and other neighbours to support your case.

- *BONFIRES:* As with noise, so with smells. You can't complain about the occasional bonfire; only if it's every day and extraordinarily smoky might there be any legal remedy. But 'proving' such a nuisance is notoriously difficult. Better by far to settle it over a pint or a cup of coffee.

- *FOOTBALLS:* Could be a stalemate here. Technically you are trespassing if you climb over to get back a ball. And at the same time, your neighbour is not obliged by law to return it. But it doesn't become his property. So it's up to you both to come to some understanding.

- *TREES:* If branches of a neighbour's tree get in your way and he won't prune, the law lets you lop off the branches on your side. But the wood isn't your property so strictly speaking you should hand it back!

- *THE DRIVE:* If his car blocks your driveway call him out if you want a scene, but don't snap his windscreen wipers off or you could find yourself facing a charge for criminal damage.

- *CATS AND DOGS:* Whatever you may think to the contrary, the law does not regard cats, or dogs for that matter, as wild or dangerous. Proving that the 'nuisance' caused by the animal next door is unreasonable could be extremely difficult. But for a noisy dog you can ask the environmental health department or the police for advice, and get other troubled neighbours to complain too. If you feel the animal is being mistreated contact the RSPCA or SSPCA (sometimes under Animals in phone book).

· *ALARM:* It can be an offence to let a bell ring constantly and annoy the neighbours. But if you can show it's not your fault you might have an excuse. As an irritated neighbour you might be accused of criminal damage if you tried to destroy the wretched box. Best ask the police for their advice.

· *SHORTCUT:* If your neighbours have been cutting across your garden on the way to the supermarket for 20 years or more, they might have a right of way! If this isn't the case and you want them to stop, you can ask them to. If it comes to blows you can, in theory, use 'reasonable' force to get them off your land – not to be recommended as views vary about what is reasonable. You could sue for damages if they have really made a mess – but it would have to be bad to make a case stick in court.

· *BUSINESS FROM HOME:* You need planning permission to turn part of your home into an office. But many authorities turn a blind eye to people who work as piano teachers, hairdressers and so on from home.
  See also: NUISANCE

Newspapers

If you want to complain about something you read in a newspaper or about what a newspaper has written about you, for example if you have been misquoted, or about the way a reporter or photographer has treated you, here's what to do. First complain to the editor of the newspaper or magazine, preferably in writing. If it is an error of fact or a mistaken impression has been given, he or she should see that it is put right and, if appropriate, a correction and apology printed. If you think you have been libelled, that is something has been printed about you which is untrue and may have damaged your reputation, then it would be best to take legal advice before doing anything. If you are still not satisfied you can take the matter to the Press Council, 1 Salisbury Square, London EC4Y 8AE, 01-353 1248, the watchdog of our press. They will look into complaints and their findings are usually reported. Complaints about advertisements in the press should be made to the Advertising Standards Authority.
  See also: ADVERTISING STANDARDS AUTHORITY, PRESS COUNCIL

NHBC

See: NATIONAL HOUSE BUILDING COUNCIL

Northern Ireland – Law

In some areas, the law in Northern Ireland is slightly different from that in England and Wales. But consumer rights are largely the same. Goods must be of merchantable quality, fit for their purpose and as described, and if they are not all of these you could be entitled to your money back from the seller.

There are various options if you run into a consumer problem and need advice. You can go to the trading standards branch of the Department of Economic Development, 176 Newtownbreda Road, Belfast BT8 4QS, (0232) 647151, who will deal with complaints about short measures and weights, false or misleading descriptions and certain aspects of safety and the price of goods. There are local offices in Armagh, Ballymena, Coleraine, Enniskillen, Londonderry and Newry. (For addresses look under 'Government – Department of Economic Development, trading standards branch' in the phone book.) There are also consumer advice centres in Belfast and Londonderry (under C in the phone book) which will deal with complaints and problems and give pre-shopping advice. Citizens Advice Bureaux can be found in many areas (also under C in the phone book) and they too will help with consumer complaints.

NORTHERN IRELAND – USEFUL ADDRESSES

The Northern Ireland Commissioner for Complaints (Ombudsman) & Parliamentary Commissioner for Administration, Progressive House, 33 Wellington Place, Belfast BT1 6HM, (0232) 233821, for complaints about hospital and health services, local authorities or water authority.

Northern Ireland Association of Citizens Advice Bureaux, New Forge Lane, Belfast BT9 5NW, (0232) 681117, for addresses of local bureaux.

The Law Society for Northern Ireland, 90 Victoria Street, Belfast BT1 3JZ, (0232) 231614.

The Lay Observer for Northern Ireland, Clarendon House, 9–21 Adelaide Street, Belfast BT2 8ND, will look into unresolved complaints against solicitors.

The General Consumer Council for Northern Ireland, Elizabeth House, 116 Hollywood Road, Belfast BT4 1MY, for complaints about electricity and public utilities.

Post Officer Users' National Council, Chamber of Commerce, 22 Great Victoria Street, Belfast BT2 7PU, (0232) 244113.

See also: NORTHERN IRELAND – LAW

Nuisance

The law divides nuisance into public and private. Public includes a car blocking the highway or a factory belching out noxious fumes – anything which affects the public at large. Private includes noisy neighbours and smells from your neighbour's garden. For a private nuisance you must show that not only is your neighbour noisy or smelly or whatever, but that he or she is this regularly and that it is spoiling your enjoyment of your property. If you think a public nuisance is involved ask your local authority if any bye-laws are being infringed. Start with the environmental health department (under local authority in phone book) and if whatever it is constitutes a public nuisance they will usually deal with the matter. If, however, it is a private nuisance then you'll have to resolve it yourself. A quiet word with your neighbour would be the most diplomatic step, but if this fails you will have to take legal action. At this point it is best to seek professional advice from a solicitor or Citizens Advice Bureau. Environmental health officers may also be willing to help with problems of noise even if the nuisance is private.

See also: NEIGHBOURS

O

Office of Fair Trading

The consumers' watchdog and, even though it comes under the Department of Trade and Industry, it is independent of the Government. It doesn't deal with consumers direct but keeps an overall watch in liaison with local trading standards or consumer protection departments. The OFT publishes a wide range of advisory leaflets on all sorts of consumer subjects including cars, getting credit, going to arbitration and buying by mail order. A full list of their publications is available from the OFT, 15–25 Breams Buildings, London EC4A 1PR, 01-242 2858. Most are free, but you have to pay a small charge for some. They are available from local consumer advice centres, Citizens Advice Bureaux or trading standards offices, or you can send for them direct from the OFT at the above address. It also encourages trade associations to publish codes of practice.

The OFT has a statutory duty to collect information, through local trading standards departments, of consumer practices which could adversely affect us economically or affect our health or safety. The Director General of Fair Trading is a non-political figure who can exert considerable pressure to amend consumer law where necessary.

In Northern Ireland consumer protection is handled by the Department of Economic Development (SEE NORTHERN IRELAND – LAW).

See also: CODES OF PRACTICE, CONSUMERS' ASSOCIATION, NATIONAL CONSUMER COUNCIL

Ombudsmen

An ombudsman is an independent figure who looks into complaints by consumers against major bodies. There are now ombudsmen for local government, Parliament (for central government), insurance, banking and the health service. The role of each, and how to make your complaint to the ombudsman, is outlined under the individual topics in this book. See also Useful Addresses for SCOTLAND, WALES and NORTHERN IRELAND.

One-Day Sales

At their best one-day sales bring big store shopping to towns and villages which do not usually enjoy that kind of choice. But a one-day sale can also be a way of selling low quality goods at inflated prices. Beware of sales advertised by leaflets stuffed through your letter box which do not carry the name and address of the sale organiser. If there is a telephone number, ring it. If you get no reply, be wary. If you cannot trace the organiser beforehand, you almost certainly won't be able to find him afterwards, should you need to make a complaint.

Don't be bowled over by apparently staggering bargains others seem to be picking up. Unscrupulous traders sometimes plant their friends in the crowd and 'sell' bargains to them. Some customers have been known to pay £50 for a sealed package – because they saw others apparently getting something for nothing and expected the same – only to find that they'd actually bought goods worth £5. So if you do buy, always examine the articles carefully before you part with any money, get a receipt and check you have the trader's name, address and phone number just in case.

See also: MOCK AUCTIONS

One-Parent Families

If you're bringing a child up on your own, check with your local DHSS – you may be entitled to extra help through benefits. The National Council for One-Parent Families, 255 Kentish Town Road, London NW5 2LX, 01-267 1361, specialises in practical advice dealing with all aspects of single parenthood from self-help groups to benefits. The Scottish Council for Single Parents is at 13 Gayfield Square, Edinburgh EH1 3NX, 031-556 3899.

Other useful organisations include Singlehanded Limited, Thorne House, Hankham Place, Stone Cross, Pevensey, East Sussex BN24 5ER, (0323) 767507, who will 'match' one-parent families for mutual support and help. They can also arrange holidays, meetings and other social functions.

Gingerbread, 35 Wellington Street, London WC2E 7BN, 01-240 0953 is an organisation for lone parents – divorced, separated, widowed, single or whose partner is away, for example in prison or hospital – which provides help and support, advice and information. Four hundred groups operate throughout the country through self-help schemes. Contact the national office, at the above address, for details of a scheme near you.

For information about one-parent holidays send an s.a.e. to SPLASH, 19 North Street, Plymouth PL4 9AH, to CRUSE, Cruse House, 126 Sheen Road, Richmond, Surrey TW9 1UR, 01-940 4818 or to Single-handed, address as above.

Opticians

Although we tend to call anyone testing our eyes or selling us spectacles an 'optician', the former are optometrists or ophthalmic opticians while the latter are dispensing opticians. An ophthalmic optician is qualified to test your eyes, prescribe and dispense spectacles while dispensing opticians can only supply spectacles to a prescription. If you have a complaint against an ophthalmic optician, look for the letters FBCO, FBOA, FCMC or FSAQ, write to the consumer complaints service, Association of Optical Practitioners, Bridge House, 233–234 Blackfriars Road, London SE1 8NW, 01-261 9661.

A doctor who specialises in eyes, with the letters DOMS, DO, or FRCS after his or her name, wouldn't normally dispense spectacles. Dispensing opticians will have FBDO, FADO, FFDO, MFDO, SMc(Disp) or

BOA(Disp) after their names and complaints about them can be addressed to the Association of British Dispensing Opticians, 22 Nottingham Place, London W1M 4AT, 01-935 7411.

There are some unregistered spectacle sellers who have no qualifications but can sell specs to a prescription to adults (not children or people with particular sight defects, e.g. partially sighted people).

Sight tests are free under the NHS and you can have one whenever the practitioner thinks necessary. If you have a complaint about an eye test, write to your local Family Practitioner Committee – you'll find their address on your medical card or from your optician or local library. In Scotland the local Health Board handles complaints.

If you're buying new spectacles it's worth considering the following tips from *Which?* magazine.

· Stick with the same optician if you get a good deal. He or she can build up a better picture of your eyes as a whole from records going back several years.

· If you want a change, shop around for somewhere which gives good service at a fair price before getting your eyes tested. It's simpler to sort out problems with specs if you get them from the same place that tested your eyes.

· Get prices written on headed paper rather than noting them from the shop window – makes disputes less likely later.

· Watch out for extras. Complicated lenses, tints, scratch-resistant coatings on plastic lenses and so on can each add to the final bill.

· Expect at least a one-year guarantee on your specs.

· Get advice on the suitability of frames – to fit your face and the type of lens you need. You should have the width of your face checked to get the overall frame size, the distance between your eye and ear (some frames come in different side lengths), the width of the bridge of your nose; there should be some clearance between the bottom of your frames and your cheeks; and your glasses shouldn't slip down your nose.

· Be prepared for delays between ordering and receiving spectacles, a major reason for complaint. If it is important you have your specs by a certain date, make this clear when you order. An order accepted on this basis must be fulfilled on time, otherwise you can cancel it and get any deposit back.

· Make sure that you can see well, feel comfortable and that your glasses are well made before you leave the shop. Watch out for uneven tints, check that there are no rough edges, that hinges look secure and that there are no gaps between lens and frame.

· If the specs don't fit, keep going back until you are happy that they're right. It shouldn't usually take more than a couple of weeks to adjust to new specs. Sellers should be prepared to check lenses they've supplied against your prescription. If necessary you may have to go back to the sight tester to re-check your prescription. If all else fails you have your usual rights under the Sale of Goods Act and you can complain to one of the professional bodies.

Overdraft

Usually the cheapest way of borrowing money from a bank. It is flexible – you pay interest on the amount you are overdrawn – and ideal for short-term borrowing. The interest rate is generally set at between 3 and 5 per cent above the bank rate (a bank personal loan is usually a few per cent higher than this) but agree an overdraft with your branch manager before going into the red or you could face much stiffer interest charges as well as his displeasure. How large an overdraft and for how long are entirely at the manager's discretion and, in theory, he can call in the debt at any time. You will probably have to pay a one-off arrangement fee. Some of the major banks have now introduced special schemes which allow you to run your current account into the red without having to agree the overdraft every time. They do, however, charge for the facility. And remember that with any overdraft you will not only have to pay interest but also bank charges.

See also: BANKS, BORROWING

P

Package Holidays

See: HOLIDAY INSURANCE, HOLIDAYS

Parliament

If you have a complaint against a government department, for example the Department of Health and Social Security, then the Parliamentary Ombudsman may be able to help. The position was set up in 1967 to look into complaints by the public on matters such as maladministration by a civil servant. He can order that the government department pays compensation or puts the matter right, and although his decision is not binding on either party, in practice the department usually abides by his decision. He cannot, however, look into complaints about government policy or legislation or those that could be taken to court.

You can only ask for your case to be referred to the ombudsman if all else has failed. First you should complain to the department involved and then to your MP. Only your MP can actually refer your case to the Parliamentary Ombudsman and he might want to have a go at solving it first. The complaint must be made within a year of the incident you're complaining about. The address of the Parliamentary Commissioner and Health Service Commissioner (Ombudsman) is Church House, Great Smith Street, London SW1, 01-212 7676.

Party Selling

Take a group of friends meeting for coffee in one of their homes. Add one well-turned-out sales representative and what do you have? One of the most successful forms of retailing in Britain. Party-plan selling is a variation on the 'buying in the comfort of home' theme, only in this case the home is usually somebody else's. While you relax over coffee and biscuits an agent demonstrates her products – they could be casseroles or cosmetics, plastic containers or panti-hose – and then invites you to try and buy. You place an order and the goods are delivered.

Only one person in five leaves these gatherings without ordering anything. The companies involved insist that this is because the products are good and the demonstrators have the time to discuss them, but some party-goers may buy because they don't want to look mean or be the odd one out, or because they know that the size of the gift their hostess receives at the end of the party depends on how much has been spent. If you go to a selling party make sure that the demonstrator is from a reputable company. There are some sharp practices around involving the switching of goods. The goods shown to you, often this applies to jewellery, are of a much higher quality than the ones you actually receive.

Here are a few tips if you're tempted to buy at a party: don't pay for the goods until you receive them; don't feel obliged to buy just because other people seem to be doing so; always make a note of the name and address of the company and of the local agent. Finally, find out what happens if you don't like what you've ordered or, with clothes, if the garment doesn't fit. At parties run by members of the Direct Selling Association (DSA), which represents most party-plan companies, you have the protection of a code of practice backed by the Office of Fair Trading and allowing you at least 14 days from the date of the party in which to cancel your order. Firms will also usually allow customers to return goods delivered after the 14 days are up. The DSA also operates a conciliation procedure for settling complaints about member companies.

Patients' Association

An advisory service which promotes understanding between patients and the medical services. They are interested to hear of consumer complaints. Write to them at The Patients' Association, Room 33, 18 Charing Cross Road, London WC2H 0HR, 01-240 0671.

Pawnbrokers

Pawnbrokers must be licensed to be in business. They will give you a loan if you give them something of value as security. If you don't pay up by the agreed time the broker can sell your goods, called 'pledges', to get his money back. If he sells it for more than the amount he is owed then he must pay you the difference. If he gets less then you must make up the balance. You can challenge the price and under the Consumer Credit Act he must give you notice that he intends to sell and for how much. Interest will be added to the amount you owe and although there is no set rate it must not be extortionate.

PAYE
See: TAX

Pensions
Whatever your age, what you decide to do about a pension is likely to affect your lifestyle when you retire. Here's a basic guide to what you can expect from the state, from your employer or from a personal pension plan to help weigh up the options now available.

FROM THE STATE: There are two state pensions, basic pension and SERPS (State Earnings-Related Pension). The basic pension is a flat-rate pension paid to anyone who has paid or been credited with enough National Insurance (NI) contributions by state retirement age (60 for women and 65 for men). To get a full pension you need to have paid NI contributions for most of your working life.

The reduced rate contributions paid by some married women and widows do not count towards pension entitlement. But if you stay at home to look after children or someone who is sick, you can get what is called Home Responsibilities Protection – which has the same effect as a credited NI contribution. You can make up contributions you have missed and it may be worth your while to do so to get a full pension. To find out what your pension is likely to be, based on your contributions record ask at your DHSS office (under H in the phone book) for leaflet NP38, *Your Future Pension*.

SERPS is an additional pension based on what you earn – you pay in a percentage of your earnings, up to a certain limit, in additional NI contributions. It was introduced in 1978, replacing the old graduated pension scheme and is calculated on your average earnings for your whole working life. If you want to know how much additional pension this could mean, details are available in DHSS leaflet NP38.

PERSONAL PENSIONS: Since July 1988 the Government has given us greater flexibility and choice over paying into pension schemes. We can now choose to opt out of SERPS and into a personal pension plan (PPP) of our own or choose one in preference to a company scheme. In the former case the DHSS will transfer what would have been your contribution to SERPS to your new pension.

Life assurance companies, banks, building societies, and friendly societies are just some of the people now able to set up pension schemes. You choose the company which offers you the best deal, and pay contributions until you retire. The company will invest these for you and the sum accumulated will be used to buy you an annuity – a monthly income – on your retirement. The size of your pension will depend on how much you have contributed and how well this has been invested. This is called a money purchase scheme.

You will be able to pay more towards a bigger pension if you want to – and this is tax free up to 17.5% of your earnings – there is no money limit. And, if one year you have some spare cash and want to make an extra contribution you can use up left-over tax free limits from the previous six years.

To tempt you further, the Government is offering a special incentive payment for the first six years if your contributions are transferred from SERPS to a personal pension plan.

COMPANY PENSIONS: More than half the working population, about 10 million people, are in pension schemes run by their employers. And 9 out of 10 of these are what are called contracted-out schemes – you have contracted out of SERPS and pay a lower rate of NI contributions. Instead you *and* your employer pay into the company pension.

Until now, the contracted-out schemes were all final-salary pensions, related to your salary at retirement. With this sort of pension you know in advance how much your pension is likely to be worth when you join the scheme. Now employers can also offer money purchase schemes – which don't relate to final salary.

The new rules mean that joining a company scheme can no longer be compulsory, and you can opt to leave the scheme, too. If you leave within two years of joining, you may be able to claim a cash refund. If you leave you will have to buy a PPP or join SERPS and will be able to transfer most of your accumulated share.

With all this choice it's hard to know what to do for the best. Here are a few tips:

· Personal pension plans will be most attractive to younger people and those who may change jobs frequently. The older you are when you start investing in a PPP the less time your investments have to build up, so every pound buys less for an older person.
· Before you buy a PPP find out how much its real value will be when you retire. Enormous figures may be quoted but what sounds like
· thousands of pounds now may not be so much in thirty years' time. Remember, projections for future values are a guess and past performance is not necessarily a guide to future performance.
· Beware the hard-sell doorstep salesman who will be able to sell you a pension just as some sell double-glazing. Always ask what company they work for. An independent adviser will not work for one particular company.
· If you have a good company scheme it could be the best choice for you. Your employer makes substantial contributions and although the new rules mean they could contribute to your own PPP, a survey by the Confederation of British Industry has found that most employers won't. They want employees to stay in company schemes, and many of them are already suggesting improvements to make them more attractive.

You can get further information from The Society of Pension Consultants, Ludgate House, Ludgate Circus, London EC4A 2AB, who will send you a list of its members on request. The DHSS has an information pack *New Pensions Choice – Information for Employees*, NP41, available from your local social security office, or write to Leaflets Unit, PO Box 21, Stanmore, Middlesex HA7 1AY.

The Company Pensions Information Centre, Department MM, CPIC, 7 Old Park Lane, London W1Y 3LT, can provide the leaflet *What are personal pensions?* Enclose a 9″ × 7″ self-addressed envelope and a 24p stamp.

Personal Loans

Available from your bank, for longer term borrowing, usually for some specific purpose such as to buy a car, go on holiday or pay off another debt. You pay back a set amount each month which will include interest. The main advantage is that you know exactly where you stand on payments. Bank managers therefore tend to be keen on these. But before taking one out, check about a rebate on the interest already paid if you pay the loan off early because the interest is calculated on the basis that you'll go the full term of the loan and then spread equally across the monthly instalments. And remember, the interest rate is usually a couple of per cent more than that of an overdraft.

Pharmacists
See: CHEMISTS

Planning Permission
If you want to build an extension on your house or change your cabbage patch into a chicken hatchery then you'll need to obtain planning permission from the local authority. In fact, if you're planning any major change to your property or land it's best to check whether you need permission. If you don't obtain permission when you should have done so and go ahead anyway, the local authority could demand that you undo whatever you've done – even if it means pulling something down!

If your application for planning permission is refused you can appeal to the Secretary of State for the Environment (or to the Secretary of State for Scotland or Northern Ireland). A free booklet on how to appeal is available from your local town hall or council offices.

If, on the other hand, you want to complain about a proposed change, for example the building of a theme park or hypermarket in your neighbourhood, you can do so by writing to the local authority listing your objections and registering a formal complaint. You can also write to the Secretary of State for the Environment (in Scotland and Northern Ireland as above) and ask for a public enquiry so that all interested parties can air their views. If a lot of people feel the same, your complaint would carry more weight if you all wrote similar letters or got up a petition to support your objections.

Plumbers
There is no control over who can set up as a plumber and tales of cowboys are all too common. For guidelines on how to choose a plumber see SERVICES. A good starting point would be to choose one who

is a member of the National Association of Plumbing, Heating and Mechanical Services Contractors; look out for their sign or ask for a list of members from their offices at 6 Gate Street, London WC2A 3HX. If you want advice on a technical plumbing matter to help you resolve a dispute, contact the Institute of Plumbing, 64 Station Lane, Hornchurch, Essex RM12 6NB, (04024) 72791.

Police

Complaints against the police should be addressed to the relevant Chief Constable or, to save time, go in person to your local police station and tell them what has happened. Most complaints are investigated internally. They should ask whether you agree to this and the enquiry can only be done this way if the conduct is unlikely to lead to a criminal or disciplinary charge. Informal resolutions may lead to an explanation or apology. If the problem can't be resolved this way, an officer from another force must investigate.

Some complaints have to be referred immediately to the independent Police Complaints Authority. These include serious complaints alleging that police conduct resulted in death or serious injury and allegations of bribery, actual bodily harm or another serious arrestable offence. The Chief Constable has discretionary power to refer any other complaint to the Authority. The Home Office leaflet 'Complaints against the Police' sets out the procedure. You have the right to sue the police if you feel you should be paid compensation for something they've done.

Poll Tax

A new 'community charge' to be imposed to pay for local services, replacing the old rating system. Councils will fix their own poll tax based on spending and bills will be sent to everyone aged 18 or over. It starts in 1990 in England and Wales, 1989 in Scotland. It will not apply in Northern Ireland. Some people will be exempt and they include over 18s still at school, prisoners, long-term hospital patients, people living in registered care-homes and nursing homes and the severely mentally handicapped. Everyone is liable for their own poll tax bill except wives and husbands, who will be collectively responsible. Over 18s still living at home are liable for their own bill. Rebates are available to people on low incomes. Anyone failing to register or to provide the necessary information on poll tax registration forms will face a fine but this will not carry a criminal conviction. Similar penalties will apply for those who don't pay up. Students will be registered at their colleges.

See also: RATES

Post, Buying By

See: ADVERTISING, MAIL ORDER

Post Office

Delivery delays are the number one complaint against the Post Office. Damaged and lost letters and parcels come a close second. To complain about lost post, fill in form P58 available from your local post office but remember, while your complaint will certainly be investigated, the Post Office isn't legally bound to pay any compensation unless you sent the letter by registered mail or your parcel under a special insurance scheme. But it is always worth making a claim.

Other complaints should be addressed first to the district manager at your nearest main post office then to the regional director (check address with local post office). Still not happy? Write to the Post Office Users' National Council (POUNC), Waterloo Bridge House, Waterloo Road, London SE1 8UA, 01-928 9458. There are separate offices, POUNC for Wales at Caradog House, St Andrew's Place, Cardiff CF1 3BE, (0222) 374028, POUNC for Scotland, 45 Waterloo Street, Glasgow G2 6AT, 041-248 2855 and POUNC for Northern Ireland, Chamber of Commerce, 22 Great Victoria Street, Belfast BT2 7PU, (0232) 244113.

Premium Bonds

This is gambling for people who don't like taking a risk. You can't lose your stake but gamble with the interest you would have made if you'd invested the money, say in a building society, instead of buying bonds. With a £1 bond (the minimum you can buy is ten, then more bonds in multiples of five), you stand a 1.7 billion to one chance of winning the £250,000 jackpot. While ERNIE, short for Electronic Random Number Indicator Equipment, is juggling the bond numbers your money is safe. But a £1 bond bought 10 years ago is only worth about 30p in real terms today.

Premium bonds are a National Savings product sold through post offices and banks. They are sent out from the Bonds Office within a month from the date of purchase. You have to be over 16 to buy them, but under 16s can have them bought for them by parents, grandparents or legal guardians. You have to hold a bond for three months before it qualifies for the weekly and monthly prize draws. Every month 150,000 cash prizes are paid out and most are small. If you hold the maximum bonds allowed, £10,000, your average annual payout is likely to be much lower than the interest from a building society. On the plus side, all prizes are free from income tax and capital gains tax. If you want to cash in your bonds you can do so at any time and repayment will usually be sorted out within eight working days on application to the Bonds Office, Lytham St Annes, Lancashire FY0 1YN.

See also: NATIONAL SAVINGS

Prescription Charges

About half the population are eligible for free prescriptions, so it's worth checking whether you might be one of them. Most people know that pensioners, children under 16 and pregnant women are eligible. So is anyone on Income Support or Family Credit plus women who have had a baby within the past 12 months.

There are, in addition, certain medical conditions that enable you to get free medicines, for example, diabetics and some people with thyroid complaints or epilepsy are eligible. People on low incomes can also claim, and that can include those aged over 16 and at school or college. The details are spelt out in leaflet P11, 'NHS Prescriptions – How to get them free', from the Post Office or local social security office.

If you know in advance that you're going to need a lot of prescriptions over the next few months or year, it's worth thinking about getting a season ticket. The snag is that you have to pay in advance. The form to ask for at the Post Office or chemist is FP95 (EC95 in Scotland).

If you're getting free prescriptions because of low income you may also get free dental treatment and help with glasses (leaflets D11 and G11).

Presents
See: GIFTS

Press Council
The Press Council deals with complaints against newspapers and magazines. It is made up of an independent, lay chairman and representatives of both the press and the public. It can look into complaints about published material (not advertising) and the way the press gets that material. It can't award compensation nor will it look into cases which might end in a court case. You don't have to complain to the publication in question first, but can write straight to the Director of the Press Council. After an investigation, the Council's findings are usually published in the press. This acts as a sharp rap over the knuckles to publications who don't like to have their credibility questioned visibly. The Press Council, 1 Salisbury Square, London EC4Y 8AE, 01-353 1248.

See also: ADVERTISING STANDARDS AUTHORITY, BROADCASTING, NEWS-PAPERS

Pressure Groups
There are hundreds of pressure groups covering almost everything from the safety of pedestrians to widows. Some are long standing organisations which work on a continuing basis to lobby for change and improvement; others come together to fight a particular issue and then disperse. They are usually set up in response to some overwhelming need such as to fight for compensation from drug companies – one of the most famous, and most successful, was the fight for compensation from the manufacturers of Thalidomide.

Pressure groups can act successfully at both national level, to lobby government, and locally, for example tenants' associations looking after housing rights. For details on existing pressure groups write to the National Consumer Council, 20 Grosvenor Gardens, London SW1W 0DH enclosing a stamped addressed envelope.

You can start your own group with like-minded people. If you want to do this bear in mind, whatever your objective is, that a successful campaign is based on good research, knowing the facts, having a good case and presenting it reasonably and in a rational way. For example, if you're fighting the closure of a primary school, use facts such as the number of children who would use the school in years to come, the cost of extending other schools to facilitate them and the cost of busing them there. Approach experts in the field for their help and support. Most groups are voluntary but funding is important. Work out a budget, the cash you need, what it's for and money raising ideas to get it. Publicity is vital. Leaflets, posters and coverage in the local or national press are usually a must.

Prices

When most of us refer to the price of something we usually mean how much a trader wants for his goods or services. But confusion can arise if, for example, goods are wrongly priced, double priced or marked with a misleading price that implies the goods are a bargain when they aren't.

If goods are incorrectly priced, for example an electric iron is marked at £5.99 when it should be £15.99, you can't insist that the shop sells it to you for £5.99 because a shop can refuse to sell without giving you a reason. However, if it could be argued that the price was misleading, then the shop may have committed an offence and you could report them to your local trading standards or consumer protection department.

If goods are double-priced, the shop must sell to you at the lower price. This covers the situation where items in a supermarket have two price stickers or where some goods of the same type are priced differently from others on the shelf.

The price of some goods has to be shown at the point of sale and failure to do so can lead to criminal prosecution. These include food and drink in restaurants, self-service cafés and take-aways, uncooked meat in a butcher's window, fruit and vegetables, the price of a hotel room (if the hotel has four bedrooms or more) and the price of petrol at a filling station.

See also: BARGAINS, MISLEADING PRICES, RESALE PRICE MAINTENANCE, RETAIL PRICES

Product Liability

Until 1988 manufacturers' liability for defective products (product liability) has depended on their negligence – could you prove they have been careless? But now they are subject to no-fault liability which means that a manufacturer of a product is liable to pay compensation for any damage caused by that product whether or not he has been negligent. This new law results from an EEC directive. US law has recognised this no-fault liability for years and it is partly because of the large number of claims for compensation this has resulted in, across the Atlantic, that UK law has resisted it for so long. However, the Consumer Protection Act 1987 now says that where damage is caused, in whole or in part, by a defect in a product then the manufacturer or importer is liable. The Act does not cover services nor professional liability cases, nor damage caused by unprocessed agricultural products such as pesticide-sprayed vegetables. Nor does the Act extend to damage caused by a product where technical or scientific knowledge is not such that the defect could have been discovered: this will give the pharmaceutical industry a loophole.

See also: GOODS (Safety)

Proof of Purchase

If goods you buy are faulty you do not need a receipt, or proof of purchase, in order to demand your money back under the Sale of Goods Act. But if you just change your mind about something you've bought, a shop isn't obliged to do anything for you, and a refund, exchange or credit note could well depend on your providing a receipt. It doesn't

necessarily have to be a till receipt, a credit card slip or cheque stub
should do just as well.

See also: EXCHANGING GOODS, SALES OF GOODS ACT

Property Shops

Similar to an estate agent, they help you buy and sell a house but instead
of taking a commission based on the price of the property they charge a
flat fee. You know in advance what you're going to pay and they are a lot
cheaper than estate agents but you pay whether or not they sell for you.
Estate agents argue that property shops don't get you the best price
because they are not on commission, while property shops reckon that
by charging less you have greater flexibility if you should need to drop
your price to make the sale.

See also: ESTATE AGENTS

Public Houses

Our licensing laws have recently undergone a major revision. For more
than 10 years pubs in Scotland have been able to serve alcohol all day
while in England and Wales it was only in 1988 that the rules were
relaxed so that alcohol could be served from 11 am until 11 pm Monday
to Saturday and from 12 until 3 pm, instead of 2 pm, on a Sunday. We
now also have 20 minutes' drinking-up time in the evening. Pubs, like
all restaurants and cafés, have to display their drinks prices, which must
include VAT. Food and drink served in a pub must be fit for human
consumption under the Food Act, and most drinks, not wine, have to be
served in prescribed measures. If you receive a short measure report the
licensee to your local trading standards or consumer protection department, who may prosecute.

A child can go into a bar with an adult, provided he or she doesn't
drink alcohol, from the age of 14. He or she can drink cider or beer with a
meal in a pub at 16 (but not at the bar), but it's not until you're 18 that
you can buy drinks in the bar of a pub. You can apply for a liquor licence,
to run your own pub, at 21.

Public Transport

See: BUSES AND COACHES, TRAINS

Pyramid Selling

In the seventies pyramid selling schemes were rife and some people made a lot of money – many more lost thousands. The basis of such a scheme is that a distributor, at the top of the pyramid, sells the right to sell his goods to other distributors. They then buy goods from him, at a discount, and sell their right to sell the goods to more distributors who then buy the goods from them at a smaller discount. The people near the top of the pyramid made easy money; those at the bottom usually ended up out of pocket, with goods they couldn't sell. In effect the pyramid grew by internal trading to new would-be sellers. Selling to the public wasn't lucrative enough so the only way to cover your costs was to introduce more people to the bottom of the pyramid by selling them the right to sell!

Trading laws have now outlawed some of the worst practices of this, and similar business schemes now have to abide by strict rules and regulations to safeguard anyone joining the venture.

Q

Quantities
See: UNIT PRICING, WEIGHTS AND MEASURES

Quotations
If you want a firm price for a job, ask for a written quotation. Remember, it will *not* be valid indefinitely – probably only a few weeks unless it says otherwise. If the final bill is more than the price quoted, you may still have to pay up if, in the circumstances, the extra is reasonable in view of extra work which you asked to be done.

See also: ESTIMATES, SERVICES

R

Radio

If you want to complain about something you hear on the radio, ring or write to the station concerned. Most of them record comments and complaints. If you want to make a complaint about BBC national radio, ring 01-580 4468 and ask for the duty officer or write to the BBC at Broadcasting House, Portland Place, London W1A 4WW. If you want to make a general complaint about independent radio, contact the Independent Broadcasting Authority, 70 Brompton Road, London SW3 1EY, 01-584 7011.

In some cases you can pursue your complaint through the Broadcasting Complaints Commission. Although set up in 1981 to consider complaints about radio programmes and advertisements, its scope is limited to cases where you have participated in a programme and have been unfairly treated, or where your privacy has been infringed either in the content of a programme or in the way material for it was collected. The Commission can't deal with general complaints about quality and content of programmes nor with any cases which could become the subject of court proceedings. For details write to the Broadcasting Complaints Commission, Grosvenor Gardens House, 35–37 Grosvenor Gardens, London SW1W 0BS, 01-630 1966.

If you want to complain about an advert heard on the radio write to the IBA, address as above.

See also: BROADCASTING

Rates

A tax you pay to the local authority for providing services such as refuse collection, sewers, cleaning the streets, public libraries, parks and the fire service. The bill depends on the size of your property, including the garage, and the area you live in. Building an extension or improving your house can affect the rateable value of your property so you should notify the local rating authority of this.

Due in April for the year ahead, you can pay a lump sum or instalments. If you think you are paying too much you can ask for a reassessment. Ask at your town hall for the correct forms to propose an alteration in rates. If a house is empty you don't have to pay rates for the first three months. People on low incomes can get rebates. The current rating system is soon to be replaced by poll tax.

See also: POLL TAX

Receipts

See: PROOF OF PURCHASE

Redundancy

If you are an employee and you lose your job because the work for which you were employed has come to an end, then, in law, you are regarded as being redundant. You are entitled to a redundancy payment which is tax-free. In general, to qualify for redundancy you must have worked for your employer continuously for two years (and employment before your 18th birthday doesn't count). If you work part-time you're not normally entitled if it's less than 16 hours a week, but if you work more than eight hours a week for five years you qualify. You're not entitled to redundancy pay if you've reached retirement age, are a civil servant, an apprentice whose service ends at the end of the apprenticeship contract or normally work abroad. The redundancy must be because the employer is stopping carrying on that particular business altogether or in the place where you work, or needs fewer employees of that kind. If you're offered a new job with the same employer and unreasonably refuse it, you're not entitled to redundancy. The offer should, however, be both suitable and genuine.

How much redundancy pay you get depends on how long you have been an employee with the company and on your age. The maximum number of years of service counting for redundancy pay is 20 years and you should get one week's pay for every year of service (aged under 21 half a week's pay, and over 40 a week and a half's pay for each year over 40). You are also allowed reasonable time off to find another job. These are your basic statutory rights but some companies offer better deals than this.

See also: EMPLOYMENT

Refunds

Under the Sale of Goods Act, you are entitled to a refund if goods you buy turn out to be faulty. A shop cannot take away these statutory rights and therefore signs such as 'no refunds' are not only meaningless but against the law.

See also: PROOF OF PURCHASE, SALE OF GOODS ACT, SALES

Refuse

The local authority has a duty to collect household waste. The definition of 'household' waste probably doesn't include left-over building materials from knocking down a wall nor garden waste and so they might make a charge for this. The authority can insist that you put the waste in certain receptacles, for example a dustbin or black bags, and some provide them free of charge. If you dump rubbish on wasteland you're committing an offence under the Control of Pollution Act but the local authority has a duty to provide public refuse dumps for residents to dump larger items free of charge. If you have a complaint about refuse collection, contact your local authority's cleansing department.

REN
See: TELEPHONE

Repairs
If you buy something which is defective or faulty you're entitled to your money back but often the shop will offer you a repair instead; this way they keep the profit on the original sale. You don't have to accept this but if you do it could make it difficult to ask for your money back later if the repair proves unsatisfactory. If you do opt for a repair, make it clear to the shop at this point, preferably in writing, that you still reserve the right to a refund if the repair doesn't work.

If you have had the goods too long for a refund to be reasonable the shop will be within their rights to offer you compensation instead which will include the cost of repair.

See also: COMPENSATION, SALE OF GOODS ACT

Resale Price Maintenance
Harking back to the consumer dark days of the mid-fifties and early sixties, resale price maintenance, or RPM, was the fixing of minimum prices of goods by manufacturers. It is illegal to fix prices now. With a few exceptions, including books and drugs, shops can now sell goods at whatever price they like.

Restaurants
Whether it's an annual celebration or a twice-weekly habit, eating out is one of life's pleasures – or at least it should be. But all too often poor food and service and big bills make it unforgettable for quite the wrong reasons. What should you do if you find the restaurant hasn't got your booking, your 'quiet' table for two is on a busy route to the kitchen or, worse still, tonight's salmon steak turns to salmonella by morning? Here are a few tips on how to make sure eating out doesn't leave a bad taste in your mouth.

BOOKING: If you book you promise to turn up and the restaurant promises to provide a table. If you don't show they can sue you for their loss of profit on the meal, if they can't rebook the table – though in practice they're unlikely to do this! If they forget your booking, state your case firmly, stand your ground and hope they'll fit you in. I'm afraid you can't insist that they seat you. But you can get compensation for disappointment. However, they can't refuse to serve you on grounds of race, sex or colour or they could face prosecution.

THE MENU: Restaurants have to display a sample menu, with prices, at or near the entrance to the dining area and they must include VAT. Prices on the menu you're given at your table can be exclusive of VAT, which makes them look deceptively cheap, but very few restaurants do not include VAT on all menus though it's safer to check the small print first.

HIDDEN CHARGES: These can include service charge, cover charge and minimum charge. Many restaurants add service charge on to the bill for you. It can be anything from 10 to 15 per cent. You have to pay it if it is prominently displayed on the menu and the service has been satisfactory. If you're not satisfied with the service you can either refuse to pay it or pay part; offer your name and address – it's then up to them to sue you for the rest!

Be careful if you pay by credit card, some unscrupulous restaurateurs leave the final total blank in the hope you'll add on something for service even though it might already be included in the total.

Some places impose a minimum charge at busy times. Watch out if you only want a snack or you could pay dearly for a cuppa! Cover charges can be a bit naughty, and are more common in posher restaurants, where you could pay 75p or more just for the honour of sitting down. The charge is supposed to cover the cost of laundry and they usually throw in bread and butter; some might even run to pre-meal nibbles on the table.

The food served should be 'as described' on the menu, so veal shouldn't be pork, and it must be edible and of a reasonable standard. A 10 oz steak must be that weight and so on. If you complain on the spot, the restaurant should at least offer you a replacement or deduct from the bill. If you're still not satisfied *you* can deduct a fair sum from the bill, as with service. If you do this, you should tell the restaurant what you've done and why; if they don't agree offer them your name and address and leave it to them to sue you.

If you suffer food poisoning the restaurant may be prosecuted for breaking the Food Act and you may be entitled to compensation for breach of contract under the Sale of Goods Act. If you think the food wasn't fit for human consumption, or is being prepared in un-hygienic conditions, you should report it to the local environmental health department (under your local authority in the phone book) who will investigate.

Finally, just because something is on a menu doesn't mean that the restaurant actually has to have it.

See also: WINE

Retail Prices

A retail price is the price at which a shop sells its goods. Manufacturers, distributors or importers can also recommend a retail price (RRP) but for some goods it isn't legal for a shop then to show a price reduction by comparing it with the recommended retail price. This applies to domestic electrical and gas appliances, televisions, radios, videos and hi-fi systems as well as household furnishing items such as carpets, furniture (including beds) and kitchen furniture. The point of this is to stop fictitious price reductions. It is OK, however, for a shop to advertise its selling price as being the same as the RRP.

See also: BARGAINS, MISLEADING PRICES, PRICES

Right of Entry

You might think that your house is private property, a castle barred to unwanted outsiders, but think again. At least 30 inspectors have a right to enter your home. They range from those interested in weeds in your garden – an inspector has the right to come and check whether any offending species grow there – to those on the look-out for the illegal distilling of alcohol or the unlawful training of animals.

On a more day-to-day level, here are just some of the men, and women, you can't turn away, or who could come back with a warrant and force their way in or alternatively see that you are fined:

THE TAXMAN. Inland revenue tax officers have a search and seize right without having to issue any warning to people under suspicion. They need a warrant, of course, but you won't be told about it beforehand. If you're suspected of not paying your due – the same goes for VAT – your place could be searched and evidence taken away.

THE POLICE. The police have the power to enter your home even if you aren't suspected of an actual crime. At the moment a magistrate has to issue a search warrant for them to look for something concrete, for example stolen goods connected with a suspected crime.

THE COUNCIL AND OTHER OFFICIAL BODIES. There's a great band of these, including valuation officers who can see you're fined if you won't let them in to assess your property for rates. Planning officers have the right to come in and see if you've put up an illegal extension. Then there's the environmental health officer who can come in for a variety of reasons, including cases of suspected serious infectious diseases. If refused admittance he, too, can get a warrant. The housing officer also has the right of entry on several counts including the need to value your property if it's to be compulsorily purchased. Other officials include pest officers after rats and mice, customs officers after your foreign guests, if they are suspected of smuggling, and TV men looking for those who haven't paid a licence fee.

GAS AND ELECTRICITY. It's these men who probably cause the most controversy. A householder is entitled to several warnings and reminders about an unpaid bill before being threatened with a cut-off. It's when you refuse to actually let them in to carry this out that they have the right to get a warrant from a magistrate allowing them to force their way into your home.

WARNING: Because so many officials have the right to come into our homes, some people let in anyone who asks. Don't. Sadly, there are con men around waiting to exploit the situation. Study the caller's identity card carefully and leave them on the doorstep while you phone up to check they are who they say they are if you're still not convinced.

S

Safety
See: GOODS (Safety)

Sale of Goods Act
The Sale of Goods Act 1979 forms the basis of our shoppers' rights. It covers all deals between a buyer and a trader, whether we buy in a shop, a street market, from a salesman at the door, at a private party or by mail order. Once the seller makes an agreement with us he promises that the goods are:

FIT FOR A PARTICULAR PURPOSE. This means if you ask for glue to mend furniture, then it should. Similarly you should be able to sit on a chair without it collapsing. However, if it collapses when you stand on it to change a light bulb the seller may not be liable as that wasn't the purpose for which it was intended. It's an important provision when you have special requirements e.g. a heater powerful enough to heat a particular room, but make sure you make clear what you need to the shop assistant before you close the deal.

OF PROPER OR MERCHANTABLE QUALITY. Whether the goods are of a proper quality that is fit for their usual purpose usually depends on the price and description of them when they were sold to you. For example, a clock that does not keep good time or a coat with a button missing are not of the quality you would expect. It does not matter that the clock still goes or that you can wear the coat.

AS DESCRIBED. If a dealer says a car is a 1980 model it mustn't be late 1979. If a fishmonger sells you cod it mustn't be haddock.

If the seller breaks any of the above promises, you should be entitled to all your money back. You don't have to accept a replacement, credit note or repair though the shop might offer you one of these. If you do accept one of these alternatives it may make it difficult to claim a refund later. Whether you're entitled to a full refund or just some of your money back may depend on how quickly you discover the fault. The law is very vague about what is a reasonable time in which to reject the goods so it is best to check what you buy as carefully as you can and claim immediately if the goods are faulty.

You can't demand your money back just because you change your mind or find the article doesn't fit. If you're in doubt when you buy something, check with the shop whether they'll refund your money if you don't like the item.

WHEN THINGS GO WRONG. Take the goods back to the shop as soon as possible; ask if the assistant can help you, if not then ask for the manager, state your complaint clearly and ask for a refund under the Sale of Goods Act. Ignore any 'no refund' signs, they are illegal. If the manager isn't helpful, write to the head office outlining your complaint and send a copy to the manager telling him what you have done. Always keep a copy yourself. Your local consumer advice centre, trading standards department or Citizens Advice Bureau may be able to advise you if you run into problems. If the seller belongs to a trade association they may help too.

AVOIDING THE PITFALLS:

PRESENTS. The seller only has legal obligations to the buyer of goods, not to the person he or she gives them to. If you receive a gift that turns out to be damaged and can't ask the buyer to take it back to the shop, you could try taking it back yourself or writing to the manufacturers, who, for goodwill, may repair or replace a damaged item. In practice most larger stores and chains are unlikely to worry too much over who bought the goods.

AT THE SALES. The same promises apply but the standards may be lower. For example, if a raincoat marked 'reduced' because it has lost some buttons lets in water you can claim: apart from the obvious defect it must still be merchantable in other respects. Goods marked 'seconds' or 'fire damaged' should be inspected closely before you buy them.

AT THE UNDERWEAR PARTY. If you buy something at a private party your rights are the same as if you buy in a shop. Be sure to keep a note of the name and address of both the agent and the supplier.

PRIVATE SALES, ANSWERING THE SMALL-ADS. Buying from a private individual does not give the same protection as buying from a trader. The goods only need to be 'as described'; any other rights depend on what is said between you and the seller at the time of sale about the condition of the item.

SECONDHAND GOODS. Goods sold to you secondhand by a trader may not be perfect but they must be of merchantable quality and fit for their purpose. A sofa may be soiled but you must still be able to sit on it safely.

BUYING ON CREDIT. You do not lose any rights by buying on credit; in fact you may be better off. If you use hire-purchase, you have similar rights under the Supply of Goods (Implied Terms) Act 1973 to those under the Sale of Goods Act. If you use a credit card or a personal loan arranged by the seller, under the Consumer Credit Act 1974 the lender must accept equal liability with the seller. If something goes wrong, and the goods cost more than £100, it is probably quicker to go to the seller first and if that fails then contact the credit card company or finance house.

MAIL ORDER. All rights apply. If you buy goods from a trader through newspaper ads and they don't arrive because the firm has gone bust you may be able to claim compensation from the paper under the Mail Order Protection Scheme.

See also: COMPLAINING, DOORSTEP SALES, EXCHANGING GOODS, FAULTY GOODS, GIFTS, GOODS, MAIL ORDER, MERCHANTABLE QUALITY, RECEIPTS, REFUNDS, SALES, SECONDHAND GOODS, SERVICES

Sales

Even if you buy goods in a sale your normal Sale of Goods rights apply. Many sale goods are only reduced to clear old stock. However, if you buy something which is reduced for a particular reason, for example a button is missing on a cardigan, you wouldn't later be able to claim your money back because it wasn't of merchantable quality. You would still have a claim, though, if you then found a hole in the knitwear which wasn't evident at the time you bought it.

See also: BARGAINS, NORTHERN IRELAND – LAW, SALE OF GOODS ACT, SCOTLAND – LAW

Savings Stamps

National Savings stamps were sold until 1976. They can now be cashed in or transferred to another National Savings product. They are worth their face value. Details are available from post offices.

See also: NATIONAL SAVINGS

Schools

The new Education Act has its critics but among its measures are: the introduction of a national curriculum of basic subjects, more say for parents in the school their children attend and more autonomy for schools in the way they spend their money. In law parents are responsible for making sure the child is educated, be it at home or at school, and schools for their part are legally obliged to make the facilities and expertise available. Here are the answers to some of the questions most asked by parents.

Q: Can you withdraw your child from a specific lesson?
A: Only religious education.

Q: Can you choose your child's school?
A: Yes, in theory. This has been one of the main points of the Education Act though a school will still not have to admit every child that applies if it doesn't have the space.

Q: Do you have the right to see the head or members of the teaching staff to discuss your child's progress?
A: No. But only a very unreasonable head would refuse.

Q: Can you see your child's confidential school record?
A: Not necessarily. Government proposals mean that we may in the future be able to see what schools say about our children. Some local education authorities already grant access anyway.

Q: Can you object to corporal punishment?
A: Yes. Corporal punishment has been illegal since August 1987.

Q: Do you have the right to be on the school's Board of Governors?
A: Yes, if elected. Boards must have parent representatives.

Q: Do you have the right to set up a parent—teacher association?
A: No. The head can say no, and quite a few do, but there are an increasing number of associations. If you want to start one, get a number of parents together and approach the head.

Q: What's the rule on school uniforms?
A: Before your child starts a school you must now be given a prospectus which includes all the school rules. If you accept this, and it includes rules about uniform, then you are bound by it.

Q: What about special diets?
A: You can't insist that your child is given special food be it for racial, religious or health reasons, but you can withdraw him or her from school dinners and provide your own meal.

Q: Can you take family holidays during term times?
A: This is up to the head, and in senior school many don't like it.

Some local education authorities may also set extra rules, for example to serve a certain style of food in schools in areas with a high immigration population.

Sex education in schools has always been a contentious area. In England and Wales it is the school governors, including parent members of the Board, who decide how sex education should be handled and whether it should be voluntary or compulsory. If you have any queries about it, address them to the governors. Contact addresses for governors should be on the school's annual report – sent to all parents – or are available from the school secretary.

If your child has a problem, be it behavioural or to do with learning, you can ask for a free assessment by experts. If you aren't happy with the experts' decision you can go to the local appeals committee or finally to the Secretary of State, for Education or for Scotland or Northern Ireland. Tread carefully, though, with problems of special education because once you have asked for an assessment of your child you can find your rights have been diminished. The Advisory Centre for Education (ACE) will give you guidance on special education.

With regard to discipline, a school can no longer suspend or expel your child without reference to you. If a child is suspended for more than five days a parent has the right to make representations to the governors and the local education authority. If your child is eventually expelled you can appeal to the local independent appeals committee, a body made up of governors, LEA officers and elected councillors. Their decision is binding but under certain very special circumstances it may be possible to appeal to the relevant Secretary of State.

In Scotland all problems should be taken first to the headmaster or headmistress, next to the Divisional Education Office of your local district, then to the Regional Education Office.

USEFUL ADDRESSES

Advisory Centre for Education (ACE) produces helpful leaflets and books. For a full list of publications contact them at 18 Victoria Park Square, London E2 9PB. They also give free advice, over the telephone, from 2 till 5 pm Monday to Friday on 01-980 4596. For problems in Scotland (where ACE has no remit) they advise contacting The Scottish Consumer Council, 314 St Vincent Street, Glasgow G38 XW, 041-226 5261. The local ombudsman may be able to help once the LEA or local appeals committee have become involved. It's a free service; local address in phone book or from Citizens Advice Bureau.

The National Confederation of Parent Teacher Associations will give advice and produces leaflets on how to set up an association at your child's school. Contact them at 43 Stonebridge Road, Northfleet, Gravesend, Kent DA11 9DS.

See also: EDUCATION

Scotland – Law

Although Scotland has a separate legal system to England and Wales, consumer law is nearly the same and shoppers have similar rights when buying goods from a shop. If, having pursued your claim as far as you can, you still haven't got satisfaction, you have to sue for your money or compensation in the Sheriff's Court (see COURTS). Ask for further details from your local consumer adviser, Citizens Advice Bureau or Sheriff Clerk's office. See also: SALE OF GOODS ACT

In Scotland many aspects of life, such as the education system, house buying, marriage and divorce, death and wills, are managed differently. If you are unfamiliar with the system it is always wise to check locally, perhaps with your nearest CAB.

SCOTLAND – USEFUL ADDRESSES

Scottish Association of Citizens Advice Bureaux, 82 Nicholson Street, Edinburgh EH8 9EW, 031-667 0156

Scottish Consumer Council, 314 St Vincent Street, Glasgow G3 8XW, 041-226 5261

The Lay Observer for Scotland, 30 Castle Street, Edinburgh EH2 3HT, 031-226 2503

Law Society for Scotland, 26–27 Drumsheugh Gardens, Edinburgh EH3 7YR, 031-226 7411

Commission for Local Administration (Local Ombudsman), Princess House, 5 Shandwick Place, Edinburgh EH2 4RG, 031-229 4472

Companies Registry, Department of Trade, 102 George Street, Edinburgh EH2 3DJ, 031-225 5774

European Economic Community (EEC) Commission, 7 Alva Street, Edinburgh EH2 4PH, 031-225 2058

Post Office Users' Council for Scotland (POUNC), 45 Waterloo Street, Glasgow G2 6AT, 041-248 2855

Scottish Motor Trade Association (SMTA), 3 Palmerston Place, Edinburgh EH12 5AF, 031-225 3643

Health Service Commissioner (Ombudsman) for Scotland, 11 Melville Crescent, Edinburgh EH3 7LU, 031-225 7465 .

Institute of Chartered Accountants in Scotland, 27 Queen Street, Edinburgh EH2 1LA, 031-225 5673

Scottish Advisory Committee on Telecommunications, Alhambra House, 45 Waterloo Street, Glasgow G2 6AT, 041-248 2855

Second-Hand Goods

If a trader sells you something second-hand it will probably not be in perfect condition but it is still covered by the Sale of Goods Act (SGA). For example, a second-hand dining table may have an obvious scratch but it has to be of merchantable quality in other respects and fit for its purpose, so you should be able to eat from it (unless you were told when you bought that it needed structural repair). You can't complain about defects brought to your notice at the time or, if you examined the goods, which you should have spotted. The standard you can expect will depend on a number of factors including how much you paid, how old the goods are and how they were described to you at the time.

If you buy from a private individual (not a trader), the only obligations under the SGA which apply are that the goods must be as described and owned by the seller. Any other rights depend on what was said between you and the seller at the time. If the goods are faulty, you might be able to sue for misrepresentation but you should take legal advice over this. One important safeguard is to take a friend with you whenever buying anything costly second-hand from a private individual, for example a car, so that he or she can take a note of what was said at the time.

See also: CARS, SALE OF GOODS ACT

Securities Investment Board

See: FINANCIAL SERVICES ACT

Sell-By Date

Manufacturers are obliged by law to give 'best before' dates on pre-packed foods. But there's actually nothing to stop shops leaving the food on the supermarket shelves after the date has expired. The date is meant as a guideline but according to the Ministry of Agriculture, Fisheries and Food most manufacturers err on the side of caution.

Under the Food Act it is illegal to sell food which is unwholesome or unfit for consumption, regardless of the sell-by date, so if you think food you've been sold contravenes the Food Act report it to your local consumer protection or trading standards department (under local authority in phone book).

See also: FOOD (Labelling)

Services

What happens when you have paid for work to be carried out and then it goes wrong? From doctors and dentists to garage mechanics and plumbers we use a wide range of services, but according to the Office of Fair Trading more than 13 million of us are unhappy about a service paid for in any one year and nearly a quarter of the complaints are about building work. Car repairs and professional services also come high on the list.

The Supply of Goods and Services Act (SGSA) 1982 says that anyone providing a service must do it with reasonable care and skill, within a reasonable time and at a reasonable charge. (In Scotland you have similar protection but under common law.) What is considered 'reasonable' is generally decided by comparing the job with the normal standard for that type of service. The SGSA also covers materials supplied for work as part of the contract. They must be as described, of merchantable quality and fit for their purpose. For example, bath taps must not be faulty. If you insist a contractor uses particular materials which then turn out not to be fit for your particular job, you have no claim but they must still be merchantable. If he chooses them you do.

If you're not satisfied with the way a job's been done, and you haven't yet paid the bill, you can ask the contractor how much it would cost to put it right and deduct that amount. If you have already paid the bill, for example, the fault has not been discovered in time, you may have to sue the original contractor for the cost of putting it right if he won't do it himself. For major work you could withhold a final payment (not all of it) for several weeks or months to make sure the job is done satisfactorily. If something cannot be put right, for example a cleaner ruins your coat, you are entitled to compensation (its secondhand value) if you can prove that the contractor didn't take reasonable care. If you think you have a claim for compensation, it is best to take legal advice. If a contractor causes you injury or damages your property as a result of not taking reasonable care, you may be able to sue him for negligence. Once again seek legal advice.

If you want a job done within a certain time make that clear from the beginning, preferably in writing; otherwise it has to be done in a reasonable time and how long that is will depend on what the job involves. If you agree a firm date and the work isn't completed within it you can claim compensation for breach of contract. If you didn't agree a date at the start but think the job is taking longer than it should, write to the contractor setting a date by which the work should be finished. This is called making time of the essence of the contract. If he then fails to meet that date you are within your rights to call in another contractor to finish it and then sue the first for the cost of completing the job and for compensation for the inconvenience. This can, however, prove tricky so only do it as a last resort.

Avoid paying in advance. Sometimes it is reasonable to ask for money for materials but only do this if you are satisfied the firm is reputable. If you do pay in advance do it by cheque or credit card so you have a record and insist on a receipt with the firm's name and address on it.

If you have a complaint first try to sort it out with the contractor, preferably in writing. Outline the problem and what you want him to do about it, and remember to keep a copy of all correspondence. If you can't sort it out with the trader, and he has a head office, write to the customer service department there. If you've paid by credit card and it cost more than £100, ask the finance company to help you; they are equally liable under the Consumer Credit Act.

If the firm belongs to a trade association, ask them if they can help. Some trade associations operate codes of practice backed by the Office of Fair Trading (OFT). Although not all the codes are effective, generally speaking you should have less cause to complain if you employ a firm which subscribes to one. The OFT has leaflets describing each code.

Of course, the best way is to avoid a problem in the first place, which means choosing a contractor wisely. As well as checking on membership of trade associations try to go by personal recommendation from someone who has been satisfied with a contractor's work in the past. Make clear what you want done, and by when, from the outset to avoid misunderstanding later. Where possible get a firm price, in writing, in advance and ask the contractor to contact you, before going any further, if at any stage it looks as though the job is going to cost more.

Finding a good workman in an emergency can be a nightmare. This is when the cowboys can really have a field day. If you have to call someone out in an emergency, make sure you ask about minimum or call out charges (and what they include) on the phone and try to pick a manufacturer's own engineer or members of a trade association.

See also: ADVANCE PAYMENTS, AFTER SALES SERVICE, BUILDERS, CARS, CODES OF PRACTICE, CONSUMER CREDIT ACT, DOUBLE GLAZING, DRY CLEANERS, ESTATE AGENTS, ESTIMATES, EXCLUSION CLAUSES, GUARANTEES, HEALTH SERVICE, MAINTENANCE CONTRACTS, QUOTATIONS, REPAIRS, WARRANTIES

Sex Discrimination
See: EQUAL OPPORTUNITIES

Shares
When a company issues shares, it's asking the public to invest money in it in return for a stake, or share, in its value. Companies usually do this either to raise money to expand or to allow those who built up the business in the first place to get some money out of it.

Shares are bought and sold on the Stock Exchange. As a shareholder you usually have the right to vote at the company's annual general meeting and to share the profits through a dividend of so many pence per share, usually paid twice a year.

If you want to get in on the act there are several ways to go about it depending on the particular shares you want. New issues are the easiest and cheapest to buy. These are shares not already available on the stock market which are being sold for the first time. New issues have included British Gas and British Petroleum.

With new issues you don't have to pay commission or stamp duty and you don't need to buy through a stockbroker or bank. The prospectus and offer coupon will be printed in national newspapers about ten days before dealing in them starts on the Stock Exchange. This is called an offer for sale. You can read the details in the prospectus then turn to the application form, which looks just like any other offer coupon. You will be told the application price, the minimum number of shares you can apply for and how to apply.

All you have to do then is decide how many shares you can afford, fill in the form, enclosing a cheque for the appropriate amount and send it off to arrive before the application list closes. You should get a letter of acceptance about a week after the application list closes and this will tell you how many shares you've been allocated. Sometimes an offer for sale is oversubscribed, with people wanting more shares than are available, in this case you may miss out altogether or only get a proportion of the number you asked for and money will be returned to you.

The letter of acceptance is a legal document, so do not lose it. The next step is to check the price when the shares are traded on the Stock Exchange – it can be very exciting if it goes up!

If you want shares that are already listed on the Stock Exchange you can buy through a stockbroker, share shop, bank, solicitor or other adviser who may also use a stockbroker. You will normally have to pay stamp duty on these purchases and you will have to pay for the service.

Some people own shares given them by the company they work for. More than half a million employees are offered shares in this way. With some schemes they can be cashed in for profit, in others they are held in trust for the employee.

Once you've bought your shares you can follow their progress each day in the financial pages of newspapers. For example you'll find figures like these for Company X:

1988			
HIGH	LOW	STOCK	PRICE + or −
136	113	Company X	116 − 1

The first two figures tell us the highest and lowest price for the company in 1988. The current price is 116 which is 1p less than the day before.

Shares are a good long-term investment for people who can afford to take a risk in the hope of getting a high return when they sell. They are not advisable if you need your money in an emergency. If buying it's better to spread your risk by investing in a few companies rather than risking everything on one.

If things go wrong and you lose money by picking the wrong share there's nothing you can do about it. If, however, your loss is the result of a member of the Stock Exchange failing e.g. a firm of stockbrokers, then there is a compensation fund.

See also: STOCKBROKERS

Sheltered Housing

By the end of the century, it is estimated that up to half a million retired people could be living in sheltered housing. To be classed as sheltered it could be anything from a flat in a small block to a house in a specially built village with its own restaurant, shop and medical centre. You can even buy a room in a hotel and either cook your own meals or eat in the dining-room with the holidaymakers. To qualify as 'sheltered' there should be an alarm system in each home, connected to a resident warden, giving you instant contact in case of emergency plus special design features for the elderly such as plug sockets and light switches you can reach without stretching, grab rails in the bathroom and doors wide enough to take a walking frame or wheelchair. The accommodation should also provide easy access to shops, the post office, banks, the doctor and the chemist and, preferably, to parks, libraries and day centres too. Most schemes also have a laundry-room and communal lounge plus guest rooms for overnight visitors.

If you're interested in sheltered housing, you might like to consider the following points:

DESIGN: Remember, you won't always be as fit and agile as when you buy. In one poorly designed flat you couldn't open the front door if the bathroom door was open. So, if the resident had an accident and summoned help and the bathroom door was open, nobody would be able to get into the flat.

THE ALARM SYSTEM: Contact with a warden at the push of a button is one of the big attractions of sheltered housing, so check when the warden is on duty. It's unlikely to be 24 hours a day so ask what happens when he or she is off duty. Some have relief wardens, others rely on a 'responsible' resident to take over. Others simply switch off the bells! Ask to see the alarm system in operation so you know exactly what happens when you ring.

SERVICE CHARGES: These generally cover the maintenance of the communal areas including the garden, the warden's salary and the building insurance. There is usually no way you can ensure, in advance, that your service charge won't soar, but if the scheme is already under way check what the annual increase has been in the past years. Usually you have to pay your own fuel bills so check with the builders or with other residents what these are likely to be.

WHAT IF YOU WANT TO SELL? When you sell a home normally you get all the profit but some sheltered housing schemes work differently. It's vital to read the lease carefully or, better still, get a solicitor to explain it to you. Some managements take a fee for 'processing' a sale or to help pay for major repairs. In some cases the management company takes all the profit and you only get back what you paid for your home; in return you pay no service charges at all while you live there. Also check the lease to see whether the management company has the power to evict you if, for example, you become too frail to manage alone or so confused you are a nuisance to neighbours. Clauses in leases like this can only be enforced by a court order.

Further information on sheltered housing is available from Age Concern, Bernard Sunley House, 60 Pitcairn Road, Mitcham, Surrey CR4 3LL, 01-640 5431 or, for Age Concern Scotland, 33 Castle Street, Edinburgh EH2 3DN, 031-225 5000.

Shoes
See: FOOTWEAR

Shopping
See: LASER SCANNING, SALE OF GOODS ACT

Social Services
The demands put upon local social services departments are usually very heavy, with resources often stretched near to their limits. If you think you've been unfairly treated by the social services (or social works) department or that you're not getting the welfare help you might be entitled to, write to the Director of Social Services (address at local council office or town hall), giving full details of your circumstances and outlining what you would like done. Organisations such as Age Concern, Shelter and the National Council for One-Parent Families may be able to help you with your complaint, depending on what it is about. If your complaint is about maladministration you could refer it to the local government ombudsman.
See: LOCAL AUTHORITY

Small Claims
Unfortunately not all problems can be sorted out by a trader or a consumer adviser. Sometimes going to court for compensation is the only answer. If you feel that you must take your case to court, it is sensible to get some basic advice first, either from your Citizens Advice Bureau (CAB) or from a solicitor through the fixed fee interview scheme (see under F). There is a temptation to think 'forget it' if your claim is for

a small amount of money, but taking a small claim through the County Court doesn't cost a fortune and you don't need a solicitor to appear for you. You do, however, need determination, time and patience!

No matter why you're suing, if you're claiming £500 or less, it counts as a small claim. Small claims are dealt with by the ordinary County Courts. But there are two special rules which apply only under the small claims procedure: the arbitration rule – most claims are dealt with informally in a private room, not a court room, where decisions are made by assistant judges called registrars; and the no-costs rule – in most court cases the loser has to pay the winner's legal fees which makes going to court risky, but for small claims arbitrations a special no-cost rule reduces the risk so anyone who uses a lawyer is responsible for his fees, win or lose, and if you act as your own lawyer you have no legal fees to pay.

If you want to take a small claim to court you can get a booklet from your local County Court explaining how to go about it plus a 'request' form. Follow the instructions in the booklet, making sure you have the right name and address for the person you want to sue and that you've chosen the County Court for his area. Also be sure your opponent is good for the money – a court judgment will be worthless unless he has the means to pay. Write down the particulars of your claim, a short statement of your case and what you're claiming. Fill in the 'request' form. (The CAB will help you, if you need it.) Take the forms to the court. The court then issues a summons and sends it to your opponent. (You can have it served personally, by a bailiff, which could be worth it if your opponent's a dodgy customer, but you'll have to pay extra.) He may choose to pay up at this stage; if not he has 14 days in which to reply and give his side of the story. If he doesn't reply you can ask the court to give judgment against him. He can still dispute your claim at this stage and you may well have to attend a pre-trial review at which the Registrar will advise you on what you'll need to prove your case, for example, photographs, an expert's report or witnesses. At the arbitration both sides put their cases to the Registrar in his private room, but the hearing could be in your home – if you're complaining about building work, for example. If you win, your opponent will probably be ordered to pay your court fees and most of your expenses such as the cost of getting photographs (but not your legal fees, see above).

In Scotland and Northern Ireland the small claims rules are different; for example, in Scotland a new procedure is expected to be introduced this year (1988) while in Northern Ireland only claims of under £300 can be heard, so consult your local CAB.

If you go through with a court action and your opponent still won't pay up, go back to the County Court and ask them for their leaflet on enforcing money judgments in the County Court.

See also: COURTS

Social Security
See: BENEFITS

Solicitors
The help of a trained lawyer can be invaluable if you have a consumer problem that cannot easily be sorted out with a trader. A solicitor can give you advice, write a letter on your behalf or appear for you in the lower courts.

HOW TO CHOOSE ONE: It is important to find a solicitor who is experienced in handling your sort of case, for example a family lawyer for a divorce, a specialist on employment law for a wrangle at an industrial tribunal and so on. If you can't go on a personal recommendation from someone who has been satisfied with a particular solicitor, ask your local Citizens Advice Bureau, consumer advice centre or law centre to let you see a list. Local libraries should also have a copy of the Solicitors' Regional Directory, published by the Law Society, listing all the law firms in each area and the type of work they do.

FEES: If you think you could be entitled to legal aid, make this clear at the outset. Not all solicitors take part in the scheme so check first. He should then be able to tell you whether you are likely to qualify. Information about legal aid is also available direct from the Law Society, 113 Chancery Lane, London WC2A 1PL (for England and Wales) and local offices in Edinburgh and Belfast or ask at your local Citizens Advice Bureau. Most solicitors charge by the hour and fees vary, so shop around. You can have your solicitor's bill checked to make sure it is reasonable. In cases which don't involve court proceedings and where you haven't paid your bill you can ask your solicitor to get a remuneration certificate from the Law Society or, in all cases, you can ask for the bill to be assessed by a court official. You may have to pay for this.

HOW TO COMPLAIN: The most common complaints about solicitors are about delay in doing the work, particularly conveying property. First you should try to sort it out with the individual involved, and failing that with the firm's senior partner. If you're still not satisfied, refer it to the Solicitors Complaints Bureau, Portland House, Stag Place, London SW1E 5BL, 01-834 2288. They can look into problems such as delays in answering your letters or enquiries, delay in dealing with your case, failure to deal with your money properly, acting in the same case for you and for others where your interests are in conflict with those of the other client, overcharging, dishonesty or deception, failure to hand over your papers if you have asked for them and do not owe your solicitor money, and shoddy work, that is work which is substandard rather than negligent. The Bureau cannot look into claims of negligence, claims that your solicitor has made a mistake which has lost you money. These should be made to the Law Society, who can arbitrate between both parties, or you can sue your solicitor for compensation in the courts. The Bureau can, however, put you in touch with another solicitor who will give you one hour's free advice to help sort out your claim of negligence.

The Bureau will investigate complaints and, if necessary, take disciplinary action against the solicitor. They cannot award compensation but they can order your solicitor to reduce the bill or correct any mistake if his or her work is below standard.

The Solicitors Complaints Bureau does not operate in Scotland or Northern Ireland. Take your complaint directly to the appropriate Law Society.

The vast majority of solicitors comply with the strict rules of behaviour set by the Law Society. If your solicitor has been in breach of the rules of professional conduct he may be dealt with by the Bureau or, in serious cases, reported to the Solicitors Disciplinary Tribunal. In cases of dishonesty, to protect consumers, the Law Society set up a compensation fund to repay money a solicitor cannot repay. If you think you could be entitled to this, write to the Bureau.

If you are not happy with the way your complaint was investigated, you can write to the Lay Observer. He can't look at the complaint itself but will look at how the investigation has been handled.

See also: FIXED FEE INTERVIEW, GREEN FORM SCHEME, LAW CENTRES, LAW SOCIETY, LAWYERS, LAY OBSERVERS, LEGAL AID

Stockbrokers

Stockbrokers traditionally deal with stocks and shares but many firms are now offering a full investment service giving advice on a range of investments. Brokers are strictly regulated by the Stock Exchange and have to pass exams before they can practise. They have to adhere to a strict code of conduct.

If you're looking for a broker who will take private clients, try to go by personal recommendation from someone who has used one and don't dismiss the idea of a local broker; he or she will still have access to all important financial information and is likely to be cheaper than a City broker. For the small investor, you may get a more personal service this way. There are firms of stockbrokers all over the country so don't think you're limited to the one square mile of the City of London.

Since 1986 fixed commission charges have disappeared and brokers are free to negotiate their own terms and conditions with clients. If you're thinking of entering the stocks and shares game, shop around for the best deal as commission rates are now more competitive than ever before.

If you're not satisfied with your broker tell him and give him the chance to put it right. If that fails, write to the firm's senior partner. If you're still not happy with the outcome write to the Deputy Chairman of the Stock Exchange, Old Broad Street, London EC2N 1HP, 01-588 2355 and ask him to investigate. Under the Financial Services Act 1986 there is also a compensation fund to make good any losses to the public if a stockbroker should fail. A broker can be disciplined or even expelled from the Stock Exchange for disgraceful or dishonourable conduct.

See also: SHARES

Stolen Goods

If you, unknowingly, buy goods which turn out to be stolen then you have no more right to them than the person who sold them to you. The goods are still the property of the original owner, who is entitled to have them back. However, you can claim your money back from the seller – if you can find him. There is one exception to this rule – goods bought in a public market or auction. But as the law is complicated, if you find yourself involved with stolen property, seek legal advice.

Students

Staying solvent isn't easy living on a student grant but here are a few tips to help you balance the books:

GETTING A GRANT: Grants are awarded by local authorities (or the Scottish Education Department) and usually cover tuition fees and money to live on during term time and the Christmas and Easter vacations. For full details read 'Grants to Students', a free Department of Education booklet, available from your local education authority. Seventy per cent of parents are expected to make a contribution towards their child's grant, how much depends on their income.

SOCIAL SECURITY: Most students are entitled to benefits during the summer. Check with the DHSS or your student welfare officer.

BANKS: Banks offer students a tempting array of free gifts, special discounts and so on hoping to persuade them to open an account. The theory is that the student will then stay with that bank for life. When choosing your new bank ask about free banking when overdrawn, overdraft facilities, when they'll give you a cheque guarantee card, credit and cashpoint cards; and remember, a sympathetic bank manager is worth his weight in gold.

ACCOMMODATION: According to the National Union of Students, the average student on a full grant spends 80 per cent of income on accommodation and food. Many use private rented accommodation, but, if you do, expect high rents and to pay a deposit and rent in advance. Check the terms of your agreement, including who pays for rates and repairs, with experts such as your student accommodation officer, local Citizens Advice Bureau or housing aid centre. Colleges usually offer their own accommodation either full board or self catering. Costs vary dramatically so it's worth looking at the NUS Accommodation Costs Survey, available for a few pounds from the NUS. Ask your accommodation officer about lodgings and hostels, council housing and housing association property.

DISCOUNTS: As a student there are many discounts and concessions to be had. To make the most of them buy an International Student Identity Card (ISIC) from your student travel office; this can lead to concessions on entrance to many museums, art galleries, cinemas, theatres and other places of interest both here and abroad. It also gives you free membership of the International and National Student Discount Scheme (INYSDS) with around 10 per cent discount at many shops, restaurants, garages, clubs and subscriptions to some magazines. Equipped with ISIC you can buy a Young Person's Railcard, whatever your age, which gives cheap travel on British Rail, buy a Student Coach Card for cheap coach travel, save on international air fares from London and other cities, get up to 50 per cent reduction on train fares from the UK to around 2,000 points in Europe, if you're under 26, and claim discounts on ferries from Britain to Europe and on international bus fares.

Sunday Trading

Recent attempts to update our Sunday trading laws have so far been defeated but we can expect change in the future. Sunday trading is legal in Scotland. The current laws in England, Wales and Northern Ireland stem from the Shops Act 1950 and the Shops Act (NI) 1946. On a Sunday a trader may sell: meals or refreshments to eat on the premises or to take away but not (except in Northern Ireland) fish and chips from a fish and chip shop; newly cooked food; minerals, squashes, sweets and ice-cream; flowers, fruit and vegetables (but not tinned or bottled); milk and cream, except tinned or dried; medical products at a chemist; motor or cycle accessories; tobacco; newspapers and magazines; books and stationery at railway stations, bus stations and airports; guide books and souvenirs at most sightseeing places; passport photographs; sports equipment; and food for livestock at a farm or riding stables.

There are also some special circumstances which allow further trading on a Sunday and they include trading: until 2 pm if the owner or manager of the shop is Jewish and closes all day Saturday because he objects to working on the Jewish sabbath; until 2 pm in parts of inner London where street markets have been established since before 1936; at holiday resorts on 18 Sundays a year to sell food, beach and fishing gear, photographic goods, toys, souvenirs, fancy goods, books, stationery and postcards if the local authority agrees; in areas where the local authority has made an exemption order, bread, fish and groceries; at a farm selling its own produce or a craft worker selling handicrafts from his home provided he has a certificate from the local authority giving him permission to trade on a Sunday.

If you buy something which is not permitted you aren't committing an offence; only the trader is acting illegally by selling it to you.

Supply of Goods and Services Act
See: SERVICES

Surveyors

Anyone practising as a chartered surveyor must be a member of the Royal Institute of Chartered Surveyors and subject to their rules of professional conduct. If you have a complaint about a surveyor which you cannot sort out with him, you should write to the professional practice department, the Royal Institute of Chartered Surveyors, 12 Great George Street, Parliament Square, London SW1P 3AD, 01-222 7000 outlining the problem. The Institute will look into the matter and, if necessary, discipline the surveyor. They cannot award compensation; for this you would have to take legal action.

If you have a survey done which you feel was not carried out properly, you may be able to sue the surveyor for breach of contract. Under the Supply of Goods and Services Act a service must be carried out to a reasonable standard.

See also: ESTATE AGENTS

T

Tax

While tax evasion is illegal, tax avoidance is a legitimate and economically sensible way of making sure that you pay no more to the taxman than you have to by law. There are three main taxes which affect private individuals: income tax, inheritance tax (formerly capital transfer tax) and capital gains tax. The first is paid by most people, except those on very low incomes, on earnings and income from investments though some income is tax-free (ask your tax adviser about these). Capital gains is paid on the profit you make when you sell something valuable, for example a house, and inheritance tax could be payable if you give something of value away to someone either during your lifetime or when you die. The laws on inheritance tax are quite complicated but there are legitimate ways to reduce the amount paid or even avoid it altogether. For further advice see a solicitor who specialises in tax matters or an accountant.

When it comes to income tax most of us pay through PAYE, pay as you earn. The taxman gives each of us a coding which tells our employer

how much money he should stop out of our wages to pay direct to him. The main thing to remember is to claim all your personal allowances and entitlements. Allowances include those for a single person, a married man, an earning wife, plus extras for, among other things, age and blindness. You may also be able to set off other expenses against tax including the cost of special clothing necessary for your job.

If your circumstances change it is up to you to tell the taxman so that he can adjust your tax bill. You can ask for a tax return form from your local tax office (under Inland Revenue in the phone book). If you want to query the taxman's assessment you have 30 days in which to appeal in writing to the tax office. If you have failed to claim some of your allowances for previous years, you may still be able to offset them against future bills so ask your local tax office about this. If you owe tax, you could have to pay interest on it and could also face a fine.

It's impossible to go into much detail on tax in this book – in fact it would make a book on its own – so here are just a few hints to help you get a fair tax deal and details on where to go for further help and advice:
· Stay in control of your tax affairs. Don't assume that just because the taxman gives you a tax code or says that you owe him a certain sum the information is right. Always check the details.
· Don't leave tax owing and hope that it'll go away. It won't. In fact if you don't pay up you could face interest charges and even a fine.
· When planning your finances take into account what effect, for example, a new investment could have on your tax bill.

Further tax advice is available through your local tax enquiry office, and the Inland Revenue also publishes leaflets on tax.

For a small annual fee you can join the Taxpayers Society, Wheatsheaf House, 4 Carmelite Street, London EC4Y. They will give advice to members – very useful if your tax situation is at all complicated.

Telephone

During the last couple of years we have seen the start of some major changes in our telephone system with British Telecom losing some of its monopoly stranglehold. We can now buy our own telephone from firms other than BT – although they have to be BT approved – and in the future other firms will be allowed to provide public call boxes.

Nowadays all the telephones in your home can be bought. Buying can give you a wider choice of colours and designs, and without the monthly

rental added to your bill, you'll save cash in the long run. But, what if something goes wrong? British Telecom is responsible for the maintenance of the line to your phone and will repair any faults on the line free of charge whether you buy or rent the actual instrument from them or anyone else. If you rent the phone itself from BT, or buy it from them with a maintenance contract, they will also service the phone. But if you don't and the phone itself goes wrong, you'll have to pay BT a call-out fee to repair it. If the fault develops soon after you've bought the phone then, as with any other goods, you may be entitled to your money back from the shop under the Sale of Goods Act. If your line remains out of order for more than two days after you've reported it, tell your local BT office (address on phone bill) as they should reduce your next bill.

If you've bought your phone and something goes wrong, the first thing to do is to find out whether the fault is on the line or in the phone.

Get BT to check the line. Then you could borrow another plug-in phone and try that in your socket to see if it works. You should also know that if you have too many telephones plugged in at your home none of them will ring! It's important to check the REN, the ringer equivalent number, of any phone you are buying. All new phones should be marked with this number. Most have a REN of one or two. The reason is that the small amount of electric power carried by the lines is not strong enough to ring them all.

Every telephone sold must, by law, display either a green circle 'approved' sticker or a red triangle 'prohibited' sticker. A strange quirk of the law makes it legal to sell or buy the prohibited instruments but illegal to connect them to the public telephone system in this country. You can be prosecuted for using one. They are mainly sold for export.

If you get a wrong number, a crossed line or one so poor you can't hear what's being said, call the operator and ask for your account to be credited for that call. The operator will then re-connect you but charge you a low operator rate which is roughly equivalent to what it would be if you'd dialled direct.

BT has drawn up a code of practice with the backing of the Office of Fair Trading to help deal with complaints. If you have a query on your telephone bill, first contact your BT area office (address on bill). They can check the meter readings used to calculate the bill and the meter which records your calls at the exchange. If it's still not sorted out, contact your local Telecommunications Advisory Committee (TAC). There are about 170 of these voluntary bodies in the UK representing the interests of consumers in their areas (address in phone book). If there is no TAC in the area, contact the relevant national Advisory Committee at the following addresses: for England, Atlantic House, Holborn Viaduct, London EC1N 2HQ, 01-822 1690; for Scotland, Alhambra House, 45 Waterloo Street, Glasgow G2 6AT, 041-248 2855; for Wales, Caradog House, St Andrew's Place, Cardiff CF1 3BE, (0222) 374028; and for Northern Ireland, Chamber of Commerce and Industry, 22 Great Victoria Street, Belfast BT2 7QA, (0232) 244113. The national committees work closely with the Office of Telecommunications (OFTEL), a government body which has a duty to look into complaints. You can contact OFTEL direct at Holborn Viaduct as above.

If you cannot pay your telephone bill, tell your local BT area office immediately. Where there is genuine hardship they will let you pay by instalments. You can help budget for bills either by paying monthly into a budget account or by buying telephone stamps from the post office.

Telephone Selling

Heavy breathers have always been a menace but in recent years they've been joined by heavy sellers using the lines to get into our homes. Telephone selling is a widespread practice in the United States and is growing in this country. As many as one in four households with a telephone has, it is estimated, had an unsolicited call trying to sell them something. From insurance to tax advice, from club membership to double glazing, the phone provides a comparatively cheap way of drumming up custom. Usually firms use this as a first approach so that they can then arrange for a representative to call. But the consumer should beware, if you agree to buy something over the phone you could find that you've entered into a legally binding contract.

The Office of Fair Trading has drawn up guidelines on telephone selling which include the following: callers should state clearly who they are, what company they represent and why they're phoning; they should ask if it is convenient and so should not ring at an unreasonable time of day; consumers who order goods over the phone, after an unsolicited call, should have seven days in which to change their mind.

The British Direct Marketing Association, 1 New Oxford Street, London WC1A 1NQ, 01-242 2254, which represents most of the major companies using telephone selling, will follow up complaints against members and sometimes against non-members.

Television

If you want to complain about a programme you have seen on television, phone the television company responsible. Complaints to the BBC should be made by telephoning the duty officer on 01-743 8000. If the complaint is about an independent television programme, phone your local ITV company. Most companies will receive and record your comments.

If you want to complain about advertising on television, write to the Independent Broadcasting Authority, who are responsible for broadcasting adverts, at 70 Brompton Road, London SW3 1EY, 01-584 7011.

If your complaint is about the way you have been treated in a programme or that the way material for a programme was gathered infringed your privacy you could report it to the Broadcasting Complaints Commission, Grosvenor Gardens House, 35–37 Grosvenor Gardens, London SW1W 0BS, 01-630 1966. The Commission cannot award you compensation, for this you would have to go to court, but it could direct the broadcasting company to publish its decision in the press.

See also: ADVERTISING, BROADCASTING, RADIO

Time-Share

If you fancy owning your own holiday home, perhaps in the sun or in the highlands of Scotland, but can't find the cash then time-share could be an alternative. The basic idea is that you buy a share in a holiday home at a fraction of the price the place would cost outright. Normally you buy a set period, like the first two weeks of May, and each year those weeks are yours. You can go there yourself or let them to other people. They are yours to sell or to leave your children in your will. You can also swap your weeks with other time-sharers. So, instead of spending two weeks at your own time-share apartment in, say, Scotland in June, you might spend a fortnight in Florida in September. There are organisations that can help you do this but some swaps are more easily facilitated than others. Usually the rights of a time-share last a long time, rather like a long lease, or forever. Each year you have to pay a service charge to cover the cost of maintenance and repairs and, of course, you have the cost of getting there.

Time-sharing has come in for some bad press in recent times with tales of sharp sales practices both at home and abroad. Here are some dos and dont's if you're seriously considering investing in time-share:

DO – choose your country, resort and accommodation carefully. Go into it in detail and don't buy on the spur of the moment.

· use a solicitor. This need not cost much if the development company has done its own work properly.
· make sure you are being offered proper title to the property before paying any money. Some countries have complicated laws about selling property to foreigners.
· deal with a company whose ownership is based in Britain.
· check exactly how the annual charges are arrived at and how they may rise.
· find out how you can be sure you'll get what you were promised if the development isn't complete.
· deal with a company that is a member of the Time-share Developers

Association. They have drawn up a code of conduct to help protect consumers.

DON'T – regard time-sharing as an investment in property. See it as a way of pre-paying part of your future holiday costs.
· buy without seeing the property or talking to other time-share owners on the same development.
· borrow the money for your time-share abroad; if the pound falls you could pay far more than you intended.

The Time-share Developers Association also offers an information service to anyone interested in time-share. You can either write to them at 23 Buckingham Gate, London SW1E 6LB or phone 01-821 8845.

Toys

An unsafe electric oven, a toy buggy which slices fingertips and a cuddly toy with hair that can choke a baby to death are some of the toys that have been on sale in recent times which could spell tragedy for your family.

The British toy industry already operates stringent standards, as do American and many European manufacturers, but there is still a problem with some cheap foreign imports and nearly a third of the toys we buy each year are made in the Far East where standards are not as high as they should be.

Toys sold in this country should conform to the British Standard code of safety (BS 3443) and now there is a general duty on all suppliers of goods, be they importers, manufacturers or retailers, to ensure that their goods are safe. If they are not, the supplier can be prosecuted under the Consumer Protection Act 1987. The retailer does have a defence if he neither knew nor had reasonable grounds for believing the goods failed to comply with the general safety requirement.

If you think a toy is unsafe, report it immediately to your local consumer protection or trading standards department (under local authority in phone book), who will not only check the toy but take steps to get similar ones withdrawn from sale. If you can, also tell the shop where you bought it. A reputable shopkeeper should willingly take action to stop other people buying a potentially dangerous toy.

When buying toys you can help yourself choose something which is safe by:

- shopping at good toy shops, well-established chain stores or super-markets – many carry out their own safety testing. Avoid market traders.
- being wary of cheap imports and lookalikes. They are not all bad, of course, but to be sure a good policy is to check for a British Standard mark or look at the country of origin.
- checking on quality and design yourself. Are there any sharp edges or points? Are the eyes and limbs of stuffed toys firmly attached? Are all inner workings of mechanical toys adequately guarded against in-quisitive fingers?
- not being afraid to give toys a gentle 'pull and tug' check before buying.
- choosing a toy that's right for the child's age, ability and character. Many toys have age suitability marked on the pack, and although this should only be taken as a guideline, because children do vary, it's well worth heeding.
- being wary of anything electrical which is cheap and not made by a well-known manufacturer.

See also: COUNTERFEITING, GOODS (Safety)

Trade Associations

If you need a service, ask if the trader is a member of a trade association. It's not a guarantee of quality but it helps. Many business people are members of trade associations which regulate their behaviour. Some have drawn up codes of practice backed by the Office of Fair Trading, which aim at giving consumers a better deal. They usually include a procedure to deal with complaints and generally expect you to try to sort the problem out with their member first. Most trade associations ask members to display the association symbol, so either look out for these when choosing a trader or ask the appropriate association for a list of members in your area. See individual trades (e.g. PLUMBERS) for associa-tion addresses.

See also: ARBITRATION, CODES OF PRACTICE, OFFICE OF FAIR TRADING

Trade Descriptions Act

The Trade Descriptions Act (TDA) 1968 makes it a criminal offence to falsely describe or make a false statement about goods and services. It also prohibits certain misleading or false pricing of goods. The Act is enforced by local consumer protection or trading standards departments (the Department of Economic Development in Northern Ireland) to which you should report any suspected breach of the Act. It is however a criminal rather than a civil law so cannot directly help the consumer who may have been misled. However, if a trading standards officer prosecutes a trader under the TDA he may ask the court to award compensation to the consumer if appropriate. It's not wise to rely on this if you want compensation; although the threat of criminal prosecution could work wonders, you may do better by suing the trader for breach of contract or misrepresentation under civil law.

The Consumer Protection Act 1987 will soon replace the TDA in respect of misleading prices and widen its coverage. For example, it is now an offence if a price which was not misleading at the time of publication becomes misleading at some time in the future, for example a holiday brochure which becomes out of date.

See also: BARGAINS, FOOD, LABELS, MISLEADING PRICES

Trademarks

Trademarks have been used for hundreds of years. Legally a manufacturer can use any name he likes for his product so long as it isn't misleading, doesn't cause public offence and cannot be confused with another product of a similar name. Brand names and symbols can be registered as trademarks by law. A trademark must not imply patronage, for example by using the word 'royal', nor must it express a particular meaning which would be identified with the goods, for example you couldn't call something 'Cheap and Healthy'. Usually a trademark is the name of the company or product, possibly written in a distinctive way. Some brand names are no longer protected and are used to refer to that type of goods generally, for example gramophone; others are still registered trademarks and include Biro and Formica.

See also: BRAND NAMES

Trading Standards

All local authorities have a trading standards department, sometimes called consumer protection or weights and measures department, whose job it is to investigate complaints and enforce the criminal law regarding false or misleading descriptions or prices, inaccurate weights and measures and some aspects of safety of goods and of consumer credit. They are also responsible for enforcing some laws relating to food, for example labelling and composition. If you think a trader has broken the criminal law, report him to your local trading standards department (under the local authority in the phone book). They may also give you general consumer advice, including civil obligations under the Sale of Goods Act, or if they are too busy, as many are, suggest who could give you further help.

See also: CITIZENS ADVICE BUREAUX, CONSUMER ADVICE CENTRES, LOCAL AUTHORITIES, MISLEADING PRICES, OFFICE OF FAIR TRADING, SALE OF GOODS ACT

Trains

If you have a complaint about British Rail, whether it's about a dirty train or an unfair refund, write first to the Railway Area Manager (under British Rail in the phone book). If the dispute is not settled, contact your local Transport Users' Consultative Committee (London Regional Passengers' Committee in London). Check their number at your local station. Still not satisfied? British Rail has now drawn up a code of practice which includes an arbitration scheme for helping to solve disputes. However, if you choose to go to arbitration remember that the decision is final and legally binding; you can't later start proceedings in court. Your TUCC will be able to advise you on how successful your claim is likely to be.

At national level the Central Transport Consultative Committee co-ordinates the work of the local committees and usually has some chastising comments to make on rail services in its reports.

Transport

See: AIR TRAVEL, BUSES AND COACHES, TRAINS

Travel

See: ABTA, AIR TRAVEL, ATOL, BUCKET SHOPS, BUSES AND COACHES, CARS, CUSTOMS AND EXCISE, DUTY FREES, HOLIDAY INSURANCE, HOLIDAYS, TRAVEL AGENTS, TRAVELLERS' CHEQUES

Travel Agents

Travel agents are the middle men between tour operators offering holidays and consumers who want to buy them. They make their money through the commission they get from selling a holiday and that is reflected in the price you pay.

A good agent should be able to give you advice about countries, resorts and accommodation and shouldn't just send you away with an armful of brochures. For a really honest report on a resort ask him to show you the *Agent's Gazetteer* – most have them tucked under the counter – which tells far more about resorts and hotels than any glossy brochure would dare. The majority of travel agents are members of ABTA, the Association of British Travel Agents, 55–57 Newman Street, London W1P 4AH, who have drawn up a code of practice with which members should comply. Members can be fined or even expelled from ABTA for breach of the code. ABTA will look into disputes with members and operates a bonding scheme in case the company goes bust.

See also: ABTA

Travellers' Cheques

Still by far the most popular way of taking holiday money abroad. On the plus side they are simple, cashable in many places including airports, banks, *bureaux de change*, shops and hotels, and they are safe. You sign them once when you pick them up and then the money is guaranteed and will be refunded if you lose them or have them stolen. You sign them a second time when you wish to cash them. They can be bought over the counter in your bank – branches without large foreign exchange departments will probably need a week's notice – at some building societies and at some travel agents. On the minus side they are expensive – you pay in advance and pay commission twice, about one per cent on sterling cheques when you get them plus a further commission when you cash them abroad. If you bring them back you won't have to pay commission again to get your money back. If you choose to take travellers' cheques in the currency of the country you're visiting, you don't usually have to pay commission to change them once you're there, though you will if you bring any back.

To play safe, and make claiming a refund easier if you lose them, keep a note of the cheque numbers in a separate place from the cheques themselves and take this list away with you. Also ask your bank or whoever supplied them for a list of refund centres and agents in the country you are visiting.

In some countries you will find it easier to cash cheques in the local currency, for example in the United States dollar travellers' cheques are easier to cash than sterling. Check with your bank, travel agent or building society.

U

Unfair Contract Terms Act

Once you make a contract with someone, both of you are legally bound by its terms. However, in the past some unscrupulous traders have managed to wriggle out of their responsibility to consumers by putting exclusion clauses in the small print of the agreement, usually in minute writing at the bottom of the page. One of the worst examples of this type of clause was one excluding liability for death or injury 'however caused'. This in effect meant that if a trader was partly to blame for something happening to you he wasn't responsible. This is no longer the case, thankfully. The Unfair Contract Terms Act 1977 has made many of these clauses invalid; others have to be fair and reasonable to be valid. The Act applies just as much to verbal contracts and notices as it does to

written agreements. Traders cannot now limit their responsibility for death or injury due to their negligence, nor can they exclude or limit our rights under the Sale of Goods Act. They can only rely on clauses which limit responsibility for loss or damage caused by their negligence – for example a sign in a cloakroom saying 'articles left here at owner's risk' – if they are fair and reasonable. For such a sign to be valid, that is reasonable, it would have to be placed at the entrance to a hotel cloakroom where you could see it before leaving your coat. If the cloakroom was attended then such a sign probably wouldn't be reasonable. Clauses which try to let the trader break his contract with you, for example allowing a holiday company to change your package deal without paying you compensation, would have to be fair and reasonable to be valid and it would be up to the trader to prove that it was reasonable.

See also: EXCLUSION CLAUSES

Unit Pricing

Some foods have, by law, to be marked with the unit price: the price per pound or per kilo. These foods include uncooked meat in a butcher's window or supermarket, most chilled, frozen and salted fish, but not fish fingers or fish cakes, pre-packed cheese if not sold in round number quantities and fruit and vegetables not sold pre-packed.

Unsolicited Goods

Remember the encyclopaedia you didn't order but which arrived on the doorstep followed by a demand for payment a week later? Well, thanks to the Unsolicited Goods and Services Act 1971 (Unsolicited Goods and Services (Northern Ireland) Order 1976 in Northern Ireland) anyone receiving unsolicited goods, goods they never asked to receive in the first place, can keep them without paying for them so long as six months has elapsed and the seller hasn't called to collect them. To shorten this period you can write to the seller, give him your name and address, tell him that you have unsolicited goods and give him details of how he can collect them. If he doesn't then collect them within 30 days you can keep them. You can't unreasonably refuse to let him collect the goods within either the 6 months or the 30 days. It is also a legal offence to try to bully consumers into paying for unsolicited goods, so if you think a trader is trying to do this you should report him to the local trading standards or consumer protection department.

V

Value Added Tax
VAT is an indirect tax on most consumer goods and services – indirect because you do not pay it straight to the taxman but indirectly through the suppliers of the goods and services you choose to buy. There are currently two rates: standard rate of 15 per cent and zero; the latter applies to food, books, children's clothing and footwear, drugs and medicines and most forms of transport. A trader has to be registered for VAT if his turnover is more than £22,100. You can register even if your turnover is less than that; this adds to the paperwork but means that you can recover the VAT on items such as fuel or machinery you need to buy to carry out your work. If your business supplies to the trade this may be worthwhile, as your customers can in turn pass on the VAT or claim it back. If, however, you are supplying the public it wouldn't be worth your while – it would only push up your prices.

Vehicle Builders and Repairers Association
VBRA, Belmont House, Gildersome, Leeds LS27 7TW, (0532) 538333 will deal with complaints about their members' work. Members have agreed to abide by a code of practice backed by the Office of Fair Trading covering vehicle body repairs to both cars and caravans.

Voting
Every British citizen age 18 or over, living here and on the electoral register, has the right to vote in Parliamentary, European and local elections. The Representation of the People Act 1985 added some new people to the list of electors. They include British citizens who used to live here but who now live abroad. They can now vote in Parliamentary

and European (not local) elections in the constituency in which they last lived for five years after they leave. This applies from February 1987. People who are unable to vote in person at Parliamentary, European or local elections will also have extended rights. Now anyone who cannot reasonably be expected to vote in person at a polling station, including people on holiday, will be able to apply for an absent vote. Absent voters can either use a postal vote if still in the UK or vote by proxy. Blind and disabled people and people whose work takes them away from home can apply to be on a permanent list of absent voters.

W

WALES – USEFUL ADDRESSES

Welsh Consumer Council, Castle Buildings, Womanby Street, Cardiff CF1 2BN, (0222) 396056.

Post Office Users' Council for Wales (POUNC), Caradog House, St Andrew's Place, Cardiff CF1 3BE, (0222) 374028.

Commission for Local Administration (Local Ombudsman), Derwen House, Court Road, Bridgend, Mid Glamorgan CF31 1BN, (0656) 61325.

Companies Registration Office, Crown Way, Maindy, Cardiff CF4 3UZ, (0222) 388588.

Health Service Commissioner (Ombudsman) for Wales, 4th Floor, Pearl Assurance House, Greyfriars Road, Cardiff CF1 3AG, (0222) 394621.

European Economic Community (EEC) Commission, 4 Cathedral Road, Cardiff CF1 9SG, (0222) 371631.

Warranties

You usually pay for these at or shortly after the time of purchasing goods. They extend the manufacturer's guarantee for a further number of years and are usually cheaper than a maintenance contract although the cover may be less. If you're offered one when you buy your microwave, video or washing machine it's worth considering the following points. Does the warranty cover normal wear and tear? Is the repair actually free or do you have to pay out and claim back later? Can you transfer the warranty should you sell the goods within that period and is any sort of damage actually excluded from cover? If the warranty is offered by the manufacturer you should be safe enough but if it's from an outside company check that it is underwritten by an insurance company that is actually authorised to deal with warranty business — some aren't!

Warranties (or guarantees) are also usually given free by manufacturers of electrical and electronic goods and cars. Send them back, as requested. They give you additional rights, and cannot detract from your rights against the shop under the Sale of Goods Act: they make this clear by stating something like 'This does not affect your statutory rights.'

See also: MAINTENANCE CONTRACTS

Washing Machines

As with any other goods your rights are covered under the Sale of Goods Act. A washing machine must be of merchantable quality, fit for its purpose and as described. If it goes wrong you could be entitled to a full refund, or compensation; it would depend on the nature of the fault and how long you've had the machine. Your rights are against the shop and not the manufacturer and any manufacturer's guarantee is over and above your basic legal rights.

See also: GUARANTEES, MAINTENANCE CONTRACTS, SALE OF GOODS ACT, WARRANTIES

Water

If you have a problem over your water bill and cannot pay it, tell the water authority immediately (address on back of bill or in phone book

under Water). The authorities have agreed a code of practice which means they won't cut off your supply if you agree to pay by instalments and stick to it, where there is a genuine dispute over a bill or if you are applying for help from the DHSS or local authority social services.

If you want to complain about your water supply, contact the water authority. If they don't put it right ask them for the address of your local water consumer consultative committee (Regional and Islands Councils in Scotland and the Department of the Environment in Northern Ireland). They will investigate on your behalf.

Weights and Measures

Complaints about weights and measures, for example if you have been sold short measure, are dealt with by the consumer protection or trading standards department of your local authority (under local authority in phone book).

Which?

Which? magazine is published by the Consumers' Association. *Which?* along with *Gardening Which?* and *Holiday Which?* carry out independent tests and report on a wide range of consumer goods and services. If you subscribe to *Which?* you can pay an additional sum each year to join *Which? Personal Service* which entitles you to free legal advice. They will give you advice on consumer problems including helping you to prepare a case for court. In the spring each year *Which?* also publishes a special *Tax Guide*.

See also: CONSUMERS' ASSOCIATION

Wine

When you order a glass of wine in a pub or a restaurant, did you know that you could be served anything from 80 to 190 ml and pay much the same price for each? This was the astonishing result of a survey carried out by the Consumers' Association. Some pubs and restaurants adhere to a voluntary code of practice which recommends that we should be told on menus and wine lists not just how much the wine costs but the quantity, and that quantities should be standardised and in bars and restaurants should be sold in no more than two different measures. This is only voluntary, and many pubs, in particular, do not conform.

Women's Organisations – Useful Addresses

Women's Institute, 39 Eccleston Street, London SW1W 9NT, 01-730 7212.

Townswomen's Guild, Chamber of Commerce House, 75 Harborne Road, Edgbaston, Birmingham B15 3DA, 021-455 6868.

Women's Royal Voluntary Service, 234–244 Stockwell Road, London SW9 9SP, 01-733 3388.

Women's Gas Federation, 17 Grosvenor Crescent, London SW1X 7ES, 01-235 2056.

National Childbirth Trust, 9 Queensborough Terrace, London W2 3TB, 01-221 3833.

Mothers' Union, 24 Tufton Street, London SW1 3RB, 01-222 5533.

National Women's Register, 245 Warwick Road, Solihull, West Midlands B92 7AH, 021-706 1101.

National Council of Women, 36 Danbury Street, London N1 8JU, 01-354 2395.

Y

Yellow Pages

Yellow pages is a business phone directory useful for finding a local service. But remember, inclusion in the directory is no indication of quality or reliability.

Z

Zebra Crossing

Pedestrian crossings, most commonly the black and white zebra but also the newer pelican crossings controlled by lights, are recognised protected areas where pedestrians can cross the street. Vehicles must give way to a pedestrian on a zebra crossing but not if he or she is still on the kerb, nor if the vehicle reaches the broken white lines, immediately in front of the crossing before the pedestrian. Crossings with central reservations half way across are treated as two separate crossings.

You can be fined for parking within the zig-zag lines leading up to a crossing or for overtaking on the approach to the crossing, within those lines.

With a pelican crossing the driver must obey the lights, that means stopping at red or amber, when first shown, moving off slowly on flashing amber if the crossing is clear, and going on green. Pedestrians should cross when the green man is lit, but shouldn't start to cross once the sign is flashing.